AF600420

ALMS-GATHERING BY RELIGIOUS

The Catholic University of America
Canon Law Studies
No. 220

ALMS-GATHERING BY RELIGIOUS

AN HISTORICAL CONSPECTUS AND COMMENTARY

BY
Louis G. Meyer, O.S.B., A.B., S.T.B., J.C.L.
MONK OF CONCEPTION ABBEY, CONCEPTION, MISSOURI

A DISSERTATION
Submitted to the Faculty of the School of Canon Law of the Catholic University of America in Partial Fulfillment of the Requirements for the Degree of Doctor of Canon Law

THE CATHOLIC UNIVERSITY OF AMERICA PRESS
WASHINGTON, D. C.
1946

Imprimi Potest:
✠ STEPHANUS SCHAPPLER, O.S.B.
Abbas Monasterii Immaculatae Conceptionis

Nihil Obstat:
HIERONYMUS D. HANNAN, AM., I.L.B., S.T.D., J.C.D.
Censor Deputatus

Imprimatur:
✠ CAROLUS HUBERTUS LE BLOND, D.D.
Episcopus S. Joseph
S. Joseph, Mo., die 23 maii 1945

MURRAY & HEISTER—WASHINGTON, D. C.
PRINTED IN THE UNITED STATES OF AMERICA

9

Christo
Regi Nostro
et
Genitrici
Virgini Immaculatae

TABLE OF CONTENTS

PART II

CANONICAL COMMENTARY

FOREWORD

During the course of His public life Christ often recommended both to His disciples and to those who wished to become His disciples that they renounce the world and all that it contained. Thus for example He said to the young man of the Gospel: "If thou wilt be perfect, go, sell what thou hast, and give to the poor, and thou shalt have treasure in heaven: and come, follow me."[1]

Although the Gospel tells us that this young man went away sad, countless other individuals and many religious groups have accepted this advice of the Divine Saviour and have voluntarily renounced ownership of property as a means of striving after greater perfection. Such voluntary poverty has always been considered an inseparable part of religious life.

When religious renounce temporal goods it follows that they must be sustained by others. This sustenance may be provided from resources belonging to the community as such, or it may come from completely extraneous sources. Thus, when religious renounce private ownership of temporal goods in a community which possesses property in common they usually obtain their sustenance from the revenues of the community itself. However, if they enter a community which professes absolute poverty and which thereby disclaims even the right to hold property in common, they must depend for their sustenance on extraneous contributions either freely given or solicited through their own efforts. Moreover, many religious communities would not be able to support the many pious and charitable undertakings entrusted to their care were it not possible for them to enlist the assistance of charitably minded people.

The gathering of alms by religious became especially important with the rise of the mendicant orders in the thirteenth century. These mendicant religious professed absolute poverty, and since they possessed no property at all, even as a corporate group, they had no other means of sustenance except through offerings freely given or solicited. Since the growth and spread of such religious

[1] Matt. XIX, 21.

institutes was vigorous and rapid, the question of alms-gathering assumed a rôle of major importance, and ecclesiastical legislation governing and regulating its practice became useful and necessary.

The primary purpose of this dissertation is to explain the present canonical legislation on alms-gathering by religious. In order that the reader may the better understand the legislation of the Church regarding the soliciting of alms, the history of its development is also considered. By reason of its legal enactments the Church constantly attempted to check abuses, but at the same time sanctioned the practice of alms-gathering as a means for promoting the ultimate sanctification of souls and the general welfare of the Church herself.

The writer wishes to extend a sincere expression of gratitude to his religious superior, the Right Reverend Stephen Schappler, O.S.B., for the opportunity of pursuing graduate work in Canon Law. Profound appreciation and gratitude are due also to the members of the Faculty of the School of Canon Law for their helpful direction and kind assistance in the preparation of this work.

PART I
HISTORICAL CONSPECTUS

CHAPTER I

PRELIMINARY NOTIONS

ARTICLE 1

TERMINOLOGY AND DEFINITIONS

A historical review and further legal study of the question of alms-gathering by religious will be profitable in the degree in which the terms employed are understood, and thus, before tracing the historical development of this practice, one must have a clear and concise concept of what is meant by alms-gathering by religious, as well as of the reasons for its origin and justification.

Alms-gathering by religious was commonly called by canonists and historians *quaestuatio* or *quaestuatio religiosa;* those to whom was assigned the office of seeking alms were called *quaestuarii* and *quaestores.* These titles were also used in a more generic sense in which they were applied to beggars who belonged to no religious organizations. When abuses in the quest of alms became more common, particularly in the fourteenth and fifteenth centuries, these terms acquired an unpleasant connotation, and for this reason the Council of Trent (1543–1565) attempted to abolish them.[1] Thenceforth, *collectarii eleemosynarum* was a term more commonly employed; hence this work is entitled "Alms-Gathering by Religious."

During the middle ages the office of collecting alms was sometimes designated and classified as *mendicatio, mendicitas,* chiefly because it was widely practiced by the mendicant orders, which, while they professed absolute poverty, relied in large measure upon alms for their own sustenance and for the support of the pious and charitable works entrusted to their care. These terms, moreover, were more religious in tone and did not have that un-

[1] Conc. Trident., sess. XXI, *de ref.,* c. 9: ". . . ut posthac quibuscumque christianae religionis locis eorum [quaestorum eleemosynarum] nomen atque usus penitus aboleatur."—*Canones et Decreta Sacrosancti Oecumenici Concilii Tridentini* (Romae, 1904).

pleasant connotation commonly associated with the word "begging."[2] St. Bonaventure (1221–1274) defined *paupertas quoad mendicitatem* or *mendicitas pro Christo* in the following words: *Voco mendicare eleemosynarum quaerere seu de quotidianis eleemosynis vivere.*[3]

The precise word *quaestuatio* is not found in the Code of Canon Law. The Code employs the following expressions: *eleemosynas quaerere,*[4] *stipem petere,*[5] *stipem quaeritare,*[6] *stipem colligere,*[7] *stipem cogere.*[8] However, canonists still employ the term *quaestuatio* when discussing ecclesiastical legislation governing alms-gathering by religious. Its English equivalent has been variously given as religious quest, begging,[9] collecting of alms by religious,[10] alms-seeking.[11] A definition of alms-gathering by religious can perhaps best be formulated from a consideration not only of the present legislation in the Code of Canon Law,[12] but also of the decree *Singulari quidem,* issued by the Sacred Congregation of Bishops and Regulars on March 27, 1896,[13] and of a later decree, *De eleemosynis colligendis,* issued by the Sacred Congregation of Religious on November 21, 1908.[14]

In accord with these sources, *quaestuatio,* alms-gathering by re-

---

[2] Felder, *The Ideals of St. Francis of Assisi* (translated by Berchmans Bittle, New York, Cincinnati, Chicago: Benziger Brothers, 1925), p. 143.

[3] *Opera Omnia* (8 vols., Ad Claras Aquas, 1882–1898), V, *De Perfectione Evangelica,* Quaest. II, art. 2, 134.

[4] Canon 621, § 2.

[5] Canon 622, § 1.

[6] Canon 622, § 2.

[7] Canon 623.

[8] Canon 1503.

[9] C. Augustine, *A Commentary on the New Code of Canon Law* (8 vols., Vol. III, 2. ed., St. Louis: Herder Book Co., 1919), III, 346.

[10] Woywod, *A Practical Commentary on the Code of Canon Law* (2 vols., 2. ed., New York: Joseph F. Wagner, Inc., 1926), I, 269.

[11] O'Brien, *The Exemption of Religious in Church Law* (Milwaukee: Bruce Publishing Co., 1942), p. 247.

[12] Canons 621–624.

[13] *Acta Sanctae Sedis* (41 vols., Romae, 1865–1908), XXVIII (1895–1896), 555–558. Hereafter cited *ASS.*

[14] *Acta Apostolicae Sedis, Commentarium Officiale* (Romae 1909–), I (1909), 153–156. Hereafter cited *AAS.*

ligious, may be defined in the juridical and technical sense as a privilege granted to religious institutes whereby their members either personally or through others go from place to place seeking alms for their sustenance and for the promotion of the pious and charitable works entrusted to their care.[15]

Alms-gathering by religious, as outlined in the Code and in the decrees of the Holy See, is of a definite type. It by no means embraces all modes of enlisting aid.[16] It entails:

1. A privilege granted by common law to mendicant orders which are such in name and in fact, and by special apostolic indult and the permission of the local Ordinary to other orders and congregations according to the provisions of law. In the case of truly mendicant orders this privilege is also considered a juridical right.[17]

2. A going from place to place, from house to house, or any similar manner of publicly and generally soliciting alms not from a few definite persons but from many persons.[18] The precise concept therefore involves a plurality of persons from whom alms are sought, at least in the intention of the religious. It does not include those instances where religious approach a few definite

---

[15] "Ius canonicum nomine quaestuationis intelligit istum modum collectionis, ut aliquis ipse circumeat et frequentet domos benefactorum ad eleemosynam colligendam aut mendicet ostiatim pro se vel pro aliis personis vel pro aliquo opere."—Schaefer, *De Religiosis ad Normam Codicis Iuris Canonici* (3. ed., Romae: S.A.L.E.R., 1940), n. 428. (Hereafter cited as *De Religious.*) Wernz-Vidal, *Ius Canonicum ad Codicis Normam Exactum* (7 vols. in 8, Romae: apud aedes Universitatis Gregorianae, 1923–1938), V, n. 438 give a similar definition. (Their work is hereafter cited as *Ius Canonicum.*) Cf. Chelodi, *Ius de Personis iuxta Codicem Iuris Canonici* (ed. altera a Sac. Ernesto Bentagnolli recognita et aucta Tridenti: Libr. Edit. Tridentum, 1927), n. 283 (Hereafter cited as *Ius de Personis*); Vermeersch-Creusen, *Epitome Iuris Canonici cum Commentariis ad Scholas et ad Usum Privatum* (3 vols., 5 ed., Mechlinae-Romae: Dessain, 1933–1936), I, n. 781. (Hereafter cited as *Epitome Iuris Canonici.*)

[16] O'Brien, *The Exemption of Religious in Church Law*, p. 247.

[17] Mannucci, "Commentarium Statuorum de Quaestuatione,"—*Analecta Ecclesiastica* (19 vols., Romae, 1893–1911), XVII (1909), 7.

[18] Goyeneche in *Commentarium pro Religiosis* (Romae, 1920–; ab anno 1935: *Commentarium pro Religiosis et Missionariis*), XI (1930), 81–82. Hereafter cited as *CpR* and *CpRM*.

persons, or even a certain number of specified persons, from whom for special definite reasons they may expect to receive assistance.[19] Nor do such religious solicit alms in the technical sense who repeatedly return to certain benefactors with the hope of obtaining new alms.[20]

Alms-gathering in the juridical sense does include those instances in which religious receive a list or catalogue of names of persons who have the reputation of being liberal and charitably minded towards pious causes, and then approach these designated persons for the purpose of soliciting alms. It makes no difference whether such lists of names be obtained gratuitously or through the payment of a specified price.[21]

3. An oral petitioning addressed by one person to another. Ecclesiastical legislation governing this form of alms-gathering does not include other forms whereby aid may be obtained, such as the sending of written or printed circular letters through the mails,[22] offertory collections taken up in church or in other places, even though previously announced, the use of charity boxes placed in the entrance of a church or oratory, and similar methods.[23]

Neither does the juridic concept of alms-gathering apply to subscriptions obtained through Catholic papers and periodicals, nor to institutions of lotteries even if connected with chance-selling. This latter method and also other forms of soliciting aid, though not forbidden by the common law, may nevertheless be

---

[19] "Colligere namque aliquas eleemosynas apud paucos vel selectos religionis benefactores, non est proprie quaestuatio."—Fanfani, *De Iure Religiosorum ad Normam Codicis Iuris Canonici* (2. ed., Taurini-Romae: Marietti, 1925), n. 357 (Hereafter cited as *De Iure Religiosorum*). Cf. Mannucci, "De Iure et Ratione Quaestuandi,"—*Analecta Ecclesiastica*, XVII (1909), 72.

[20] Beste, *Introductio in Codicem* (editio altera, Collegeville, Minnesota: St. John's Abbey Press, 1944), p. 422.

[21] Vermeersch-Creusen, *Epitome Iuris Canonici*, I, n. 781.

[22] "Quae enim fit litteris, schedulis aut alio modo non est proprie quaestuatio."—Fanfani, *De Iure Religiosorum*, n. 357; cf. Wernz-Vidal, *Ius Canonicum*, V, n. 438; decretum, "*Singulari quidem*," 27 mart. 1896—*ASS* (1895-1896), 555-558, n. IV.

[23] Schaefer, *De Religiosis*, n. 428.

prohibited by legitimate ecclesiastical superiors for other good reasons.[24]

4. The actual collecting of the alms by the members of the religious institute itself when there is question of men religious.[25] In religious institutes of women alms-gathering may be exercised through other trustworthy persons designated by the local Ordinary. In fact this method of procedure is preferred by the Sacred Congregation of Religious. In the decree *Singulari quidem* of March 27, 1896,[26] the Sacred Congregation of Bishops and Regulars ordained that, only when sufficient support cannot be obtained in this manner, may permission be given to sisters to solicit alms personally.

5. That the alms be solicited and used exclusively for the sustenance of the religious community, or for its needs and the promotion of pious and charitable works entrusted to its care. Legislation for the collecting of alms by methods other than alms-gathering, considered in its juridical and technical sense, and for pious and ecclesiastical causes extraneous to the religious community itself, is contained in canon 1503.

Article 2

Reasons Justifying Alms-Gathering

The question of whether or not alms-gathering by religious is justified will depend largely on the type of poverty which the religious themselves profess. Poverty in the religious sense consists in the absence of superfluities.[27] In the religious state this renunciation of the superfluities of life is undertaken voluntarily as a means of removing obstacles which obstruct the way to religious perfection.[28] Such voluntary poverty has always been con-

---

[24] Schaefer, *loc. cit.;* Beste, *Introductio in Codicem,* p. 422.

[25] "Ut mendicantes praefato iure gaudeant, per seipsos, non autem per personas Ordini extraneas, eleemosynas colligere debent."—Decretum, "*De eleemosynis colligendis,*" 21 nov. 1908,—*AAS,* I (1909), 153–156, I, n. V.

[26] *ASS,* XXVIII (1895–1896), 555–558, n. V.

[27] Turner, *The Vow of Poverty* (The Catholic University of America Canon Law Studies, no. 54, Washington: The Catholic University of America, 1929), p. xxxi.

[28] S. Thomas, *Sancti Thomae Aquinatis Doctoris Angelici Opera Omnia*

sidered an inseparable part of religious life. But since those who renounce temporal goods really possess nothing as their own, it follows that they must be sustained by others.[29] This sustenance may be provided from resources set aside by the religious group itself for this purpose, or it may come from completely extraneous sources.

The attitude of religious institutes toward the ownership of property, then, may be of two kinds. Individuals belonging to a religious institute may disclaim ownership of property, though the institute as such continues to own; or also the institute itself may renounce completely the right to own. When a religious renounces private ownership of temporal goods in a community which possesses property held in common, he obtains his sustenance through the endowments of one kind or another which his community has set aside for that purpose. However, if he enters a community which professes absolute poverty, and which thereby disclaims even the right to hold property in common, he must depend for his sustenance on small and almost daily benefactions freely given, or solicited through his own efforts.[30]

Religious poverty under both these forms has always been practiced and approved in the Church. Christ by example [31] practiced poverty, and by word [32] recommended it to others. Nevertheless Christ did not institute any detailed regulations as to how poverty was to be practiced.[33] It cannot be said that He required absolute poverty, nor can it be said that He forbade it.

Iussu Impensaque Leonis XIII, P.M. Edita (Romae: 1882-), *Contra Gentiles* (Romae, 1882), lib. III, c. 133; Suarez, *Opera Omnia* (ed. nova, 28 vols., Parisiis, 1856–1861), XVI, *De Paupertate*, lib. VIII, c. 7 (Hereafter cited as *De Paupertate*).

[29] S. Bonaventura, *Opera Omnia,* VIII, *Apologia Pauperum,* c. 7, n. 4 (Hereafter cited as *Apologia Pauperum*).

[30] S. Bonaventura, *loc. cit.*

[31] But Jesus said to him, "The foxes have dens, and the birds of the air have nests; but the Son of Man has nowhere to lay his head."—Matt. VIII, 20; cf. Luke, IX, 58; I Tim. VI, 8.

[32] Jesus said to him, "If thou wilt be perfect, go, sell what thou hast, and give to the poor, and thou shalt have treasure in heaven; and come, follow me."—Matt. XIX, 21.

[33] Cf. Turner, *The Vow of Poverty,* pp. xxxi–xxxiv and pp. 1–4.

Prior to the thirteenth century it was taken for granted that religious life required only the renunciation of the rights of private ownership. The right of religious communities to possess and control property was recognized by Church law, and was unquestioned in civil law.[34] It was not, then, a practice which was merely tolerated by the Church. The fact that many works were written during the thirteenth century in defense of religious institutes which renounced both private and common ownership does not constitute a condemnation of those communities which possessed property in common.[35]

It is quite obvious that for religious communities which profess absolute poverty the continuous receipt of alms becomes a necessity. In other religious institutes the appeal for alms may be made only under specified conditions and for justifiable reasons.[36] In either case the motive for which the alms is sought is a very important factor. St. Thomas (1226–1274)[37] describes a twofold motive which may prompt the solicitation of alms. One of these motives is both lawful and commendable, but the other cannot be justified. If a person is motivated merely by a desire of gain, or by the desire of living in indolence at the expense of others, his appeal for alms is unlawful, and cannot be justified. Such a person is little better than a thief. On the other hand, if the appeal is based on necessity or usefulness, then it is permissible and does not violate good morals or the teachings of Christ and the Church. For example, the destitute may always beg and accept aid, but the indolent may not.

One who is promoting a charitable or religious enterprise for

---

[34] McManus, *The Administration of Temporal Goods in Religious Institutes* (Catholic University of America Canon Law Studies, no. 109, Washington: The Catholic University of America, 1937), p. 17.

[35] The following works of St. Thomas were written professedly in defense of religious orders renouncing common and private property: Opusculum I: *Contra impugnantes Dei cultum et religionem;* Opusculum II: *De perfectione vitae spiritualis;* Opusculum III: *Contra pestiferam doctrinam retrahentium homines a religionis ingressu.* All these works are found in *Opera Omnia,* tom. XV. Likewise the entire work of St. Bonaventure, *Apologia Pauperum,* defends absolute poverty.

[36] Canon 622.

[37] *Summa Theologica* (Romae, 1888–1906), IIa, IIae, Q. 187, art. 5.

which his own resources are insufficient or inadequate, may lawfully solicit alms. Alms may be accepted for the erection of churches and hospitals, and for other public projects which are intended to serve the common good. Poor scholars do not sin in seeking alms themselves or through others in order that they may devote themselves unhampered to their studies. And since absolute poverty in the religious life does serve a useful purpose, says the Angelic Doctor, mendicancy is lawful for such religious, just as it is lawful for seculars.

A number of heretical doctrines have arisen in connection with the collecting of alms.[38] One such doctrine, which was rather widespread in the first centuries of the Church's existence, maintained that religious poverty required the abandonment of all solicitude for temporal things, even for the necessities of life. Its proponents insisted that prayer and trust in Divine Providence alone sufficed. In the thirteenth century the opposite extreme was proposed by such men as William of St. Amour (+1272), Desiderius Longobardus (13th century), and others who contended that it was unlawful even to enter a religious institute which rejected the common ownership of property.

That unworthy motives may enter into the collecting of alms is quite obvious. In the fourth century it was not rare to find monks who made begging a profession, since they were either too avaricious or too indolent to make a living by other means. St. Paulinus of Nola (353–431) castigated such indolent religious in the sarcastic verse:

Avara mendicabula,
Qui deierando monachos se vel naufragos
Nomen casumque venditant.[39]

Many of the Fathers of the Church have protested vigorously against such idle religious beggars. Epiphanius of Salamis (315–403) unhesitatingly condemned the Massalians or Euchites, a religious group who lived thus at the expense of others and became

[38] Suarez, *De Paupertate*, c. 8, nn. 3–4.

[39] *Poema XXIV*, vv. 329-332—Migne, *Patrologiae Cursus Completus, Series Latina* (221 vols., Parisiis, 1844–1864), LXI, 621. Hereafter this collection will be cited as *MPL*.

an unnecessary burden to society.[40] St. Augustine (354–430) severely censures certain idle monks who wandered about with the Saviour's words on their lips, that the birds of the air sow not, neither do they reap, the lilies of the fields toil not, neither do they spin. He assured them with St. Paul, that "he who is unwilling to work, ought not to eat." [41] Nothing can be more telling than the language St. Augustine used in another passage to describe the idleness and greed of such monks:

> By means of his extreme deceitfulness the enemy has scattered many hypocrites under the garb of monks, hypocrites who wander about the province, sent nowhere, settling nowhere, quiet nowhere. Some have relics of martyrs for sale, if they be such; others boast of their lappets and tassels after the manner of the Pharisees; others state deceitfully that they have heard of their parents and other relatives living in this or that country, and that they wish to visit them; but all of them seek, and all of them beg either the luxury of greedy poverty or the price of hypocritical piety.[42]

St. Benedict (480–543), the father of western monasticism, also condemns such idleness and vagrancy in the monastic life. In the very first chapter of his rule he describes the kind of monks that meet with his approval. He shows very little patience with those who wander about from place to place and lack stability in their religious life.[43]

It must not be thought, however, that the Fathers of the Church meant to condemn mendicancy as such. In the middle ages the mendicants were all too often misunderstood and placed in the

---

[40] Haeresis LXXX—Migne, *Patrologiae Cursus Completus, Series Graeca* (161 vols., Parisiis, 1857–1866), XLII, 761. Hereafter this collection will be cited as *MPG.*

[41] *De opere monachorum,* c. I, n. 2—*MPL,* XL, 549.

[42] *De opere monachorum,* c. XXVIII, n. 36—*MPL,* XL, 575.

[43] ". . . Quartum vero genus est monachorum quod nominatur gyrovagum, qui tota vita sua per diversas provincias ternis aut quaternis diebus per diversorum cellas hospitantur semper vagi, et numquam stabiles et propriis voluntatibus et gulae illecebris servientes."—*Regula S. Benedicti,* C. 1, *De generibus monachorum;* cf. Delatte, *Commentary on the Rule of St. Benedict* (London: Burns Oates & Washbourne Limited, 1921), pp. 25–34.

same category as these religious vagrants and idle beggars, who had been so mercilessly condemned by the Fathers and monastic legislators.

Numerous attacks were made even against the principle of mendicancy, and it was not infrequently denied that there was any moral justification for religious institutes which lived on alms. First of all the rise and the rapid growth of the mendicant orders placed a heavy burden on the generosity of devout Christians. Jealousy also played its part, for in the thirteenth and fourteenth centuries certain members of the mendicant orders were raised to positions of importance in the Church, and they thus incurred the envy of many prelates and priests. Finally, the growing influence of the mendicants at the universities, particularly that of the Dominicans and Franciscans, brought down on all mendicants the enmity and resentment of those whom they were displacing. This held particularly true at the universities of Paris and Bologna.[44]

It cannot be denied of course, as will be noted later on, that many abuses had arisen in connection with the practice of religious poverty, and sometimes the attacks were not unprovoked nor entirely unwarranted. Feeling often became so bitter that any attack against the principle of mendicancy received widespread approval. One such attack upon the right of religious orders to depend on alms for a livelihood was made by William of St. Amour in a work entitled *De Periculis Novissimorum Temporum,* which appeared in the year 1256.[45]

William of St. Amour admitted that there existed such a thing as a counsel of evangelical poverty, but he stoutly maintained that the religious after making his profession was bound to support himself by his own industry, or to enter an institute in which he would be sure to obtain the necessary sustenance. He readily

[44] Cf. Ott, *Thomas von Aquin und das Mendikantentum* (Freiburg im Breisgau, 1908), pp. 20–24.

[45] This work of William of St. Amour appeared in conjunction with all his works, but its sale was strictly forbidden by Louis XIII in 1633. Cf. Ott, *Thomas von Aquin und das Mendikantentum,* p. 23; Bäumker, "Wilhelm von St. Amour,"—*Kirchenlexikon,* Wetzer und Welte's (12 vols., Freiburg im Breisgau, 1882–1901), XII, 1585–1586 (Hereafter cited as *Kirchenlexikon*).

agreed that the Church has the right to permit certain individuals to live a life of absolute renunciation and to depend on alms, but he denied that the Church has the power to grant to religious orders as such the permission to practise a total renunciation of property.

The mendicants on the other hand had their defenders, and works written in answer to such attacks were not wanting. Even such eminent scholars as St. Thomas and St. Bonaventure protested against these violent attacks, and vindicated the rights and privileges of the mendicant orders.[46]

The reasons justifying the collecting of alms have been very nicely summarized by St. Bonaventure:

> Qui servit alteri iuste sustentatur ab illo; ergo qui universali Ecclesiae deserviunt iuste sustentantur ab universo mundo; ergo si qui sunt, qui verbo et exemplo per mundum discurrendo deserviunt populo christiano, merito sustentationem petere possunt ab ipso.[47]

Article 3

ORIGIN AND PRACTICE OF ALMS-GATHERING BEFORE THE RISE OF THE MENDICANT ORDERS

Complete renunciation of both private and common property was not practised in religious institutes prior to the time of St. Francis (1182–1226) and St. Dominic (1170–1221). This is so true that it can safely be said that this species of evangelical poverty had its introduction with these two great religious leaders of the thirteenth century.[48]

The collecting of alms, however, did not originate with religious orders, but has been a recognized custom from the earliest

---

[46] Soldati embodied all the writings of these two doctors of the Church in defense of religious mendicancy in a special work entitled *SS. Thomae et Bonaventurae opuscula adversus Gulielmum de S. Amore* (Romae, 1733).

[47] *Opera Omnia,* V, *De Perfectione Evangelica,* art. 2, n. 34.

[48] "Quod autem haec paupertas et mendicitas speciali modo servetur in religionibus aliquibus communem vitam in una congregatione seu corpore politico profitentibus, id non videtur esse multum antiquum in Ecclesia, sed a tempore divorum Dominici et Francisci incepisse."—Suarez, *De Paupertate,* lib. VIII, c. 8, n. 11; cf. Felder, *The Ideals of St. Francis of Assisi,* p. 94.

ages. Consequently it is appropriate to examine briefly the history of that kind of charitable and religious activity as a prelude to a study of alms-gathering as a means contributing to the support of religious institutes.

In the Old Testament the relief of poverty by means of alms was permitted. In fact many prescriptions of the law of Moses provide at least indirectly for these charitable aids.[49]

In the New Testament, Christ counselled voluntary poverty and observed it Himself in a most exact and perfect manner. That He actually went about collecting alms with His apostles is disputed by some authors, but St. Thomas Aquinas in a special article has collected many telling arguments from Holy Scripture and from the Fathers of the Church in support of the view that Christ was Himself truly a mendicant.[50] In any event it is certain that Christ at least accepted and lived on the voluntary offerings of His friends, for He had not whereon to lay His head, and He counselled this type of poverty for the apostles themselves.[51]

Even though the early monastic institutions in their observance of poverty did not depend upon the collecting of alms for a subsistence,[52] there were not wanting throughout all the centuries pious groups and faithful individuals who accepted the words of Christ literally by giving up all their possessions and by living on alms freely given to them or actually sought by them.

Eusebius (ca. 263–339) wrote of apostolic men who, in imita-

[49] "If thou hast gathered the fruit of thy olive trees, thou shalt not return to gather whatsoever remaineth on the trees: but shalt leave it for the stranger, for the fatherless and the widow."—*Deut.* XXIV, 20; cf. *Deut.* XIV, 29; XV, 7 and 11.

[50] *Summa Theologica,* IIa, IIae, Q. 187, art. 5.

[51] S. Chrysostomus, *Homilia* XXII, n. 4: ". . . *nolite possidere aurum, neque argentum, neque peram in via* (Matt. X, 9–10). Postquam enim haec ipsa operibus exhibuerat, tum demum verbis legis statuit firmiorem, unde et sermo acceptus et comprobatus erat, ipsius nempe operibus iam firmatus. Ubinam igitur operibus demonstravit? Audi ipsum dicentem: *Filius hominis non habet ubi caput reclinet* (Matt. VIII, 20). Neque hoc tamen dixisse contentum, in discipulis suis horum exemplum suppeditat, cum ipsos ad hanc formam redegit, et nullo modo egere permisit."—*MPG,* LVII, 304.

[52] Some institutes practised the most rigid poverty, but they nevertheless retained common ownership of property. Cf. Turner, *The Vow of Poverty,* p. 54.

tion of the poverty of the apostles, sold all their possessions, gave to the poor, and then set out to preach the Gospel, often among nations and peoples of whom they had never heard. These apostolic men owned nothing in private or in common with others, and belonged to no religious community. They lived on alms voluntarily supplied by the faithful and, if these did not suffice, they resorted to mendicancy.[53] St. Jerome (ca. 342–420) praised Fabiola for her complete trust in God, and for her reliance upon alms after she had expended all her wealth on the poor for the sake of Christ.[54] St. Bonaventure in his work *De Perfectione Evangelica,*[55] in defending alms-gathering in the mendicant orders, describes the disciples of Paul who possessed nothing, and lived in want and need. They accepted the voluntary offerings of the faithful, and on their journeys they sought alms to provide for their daily necessities.

Finally, there is the illustrious example of St. Alexius (5th century), who according to legend was the son of a distinguished Roman family, and is said to have left home immediately after his marriage and to have journeyed to Edessa in Syria, where for seventeen years he lived the life of a mendicant. There he collected alms and shared them with the poor, reserving only enough for the absolute necessities of life. Later he returned to his home, where, unknown to his own household till the day of his death, he continued his life of begging.[56]

These examples suggest that there have been many holy souls who have professed a life of absolute poverty although they belonged to no particular religious community; if they did not earn enough for their own support by the labors of their hands, they certainly lived on alms freely offered, and frequently even begged for the necessities of life.[57]

Alms-gathering by those who do not profess voluntary poverty is a consideration which is beyond the scope of this work; how-

---

[53] *Historiae Ecclesiasticae,* lib. III, c. 31—*MPG,* XX, 279–282.

[54] *Epistola ad Oceanum,* LXXVII, n. 2—*MPL,* XXII, 691.

[55] Quaest. II, art. 2, n. 19—*Opera Omnia,* V, 138.

[56] Kirsch, "Alexius, Saint and Confessor,"—*Catholic Encyclopedia, The* (16 vols. and 3 suppls., New York, 1907–1922), I, 307–308.

[57] Suarez, *De Paupertate,* c. 8, n. 10.

ever, it is noted here for the sake of completeness, since it has undoubtedly been practised at times for the furtherance of the work of the Church. Thus *collectarii* have sometimes been designated by the Supreme Pontiffs to solicit alms in behalf of the Holy See, by archbishops for the construction and repair of metropolitan churches, and by bishops for diocesan charitable undertakings.[58]

During the Crusades this method of soliciting aid became more common, for it was during this period that the term *quaestores* came into use.[59] Nevertheless this procedure was an extraordinary one, for up to the time of Innocent III (1198–1216) the expenses encountered during the Crusades were generally met by larger contributions of higher ranking civil officials, and especially by the assessments levied against all members of the hierarchy.[60] Thus Pope Clement III (1187–1191) compelled the clergy to contribute certain sums, and ordered bishops to send out prudent men to collect the subsidy.[61] The IV General Council of the Lateran (1215) assessed the cardinals one-tenth of their income, and the remainder of the clergy one-twentieth of their income for a period of three years to meet the expenditures required by the Crusades.[62]

When these sources of revenue failed to supply the required funds, alms were solicited from all the faithful. Pope Innocent III prescribed that, in addition to the clerical taxes, alms-chests be placed in every church, where the faithful could deposit donations. He granted indulgences to all who took part in this holy

---

58 Barbosa, *Iuris Ecclesiastici Universi Libri Tres* (Lugduni, 1672), lib. I, c. VII, n. 78; Mostazo, *De Causis Piis* (Lugduni, 1686), lib. VII, c. XIII, n. 11.

59 Hefele, "Almosenprediger,"—*Kirchenlexikon,* I, 576; Mannucci, "De Historia Iuris Quaestuandi"—*Analecta Ecclesiastica,* XVII (1909), 289, n. 6.

60 Michaud, *The History of the Crusades* (translated from the French by Robson, 3 vols., New York, 1853), I, 26–27.

61 *Epistola 112—MPL,* CCVII, 335; cf. also Potthast, *Regesta Pontificum Romanorum, inde ab A. post Christum natum MCXCVIII ad MCCCIV* (2 vols., Berolini, 1874–1875), I, n. 3785, and I, n. 3787. (Hereafter cited as Potthast.)

62 Mansi, *Sacrorum Conciliorum Nova et Amplissima Collectio* (53 vols. in 60, Paris, Arnhem, Leipzig, 1901–1927), XXII, 1062–1063. (Hereafter cited as Mansi.)

enterprise either by actually enlisting in the Crusade or by aiding it in a material way.[63] In a letter to the bishop of Ratisbon, Innocent III recommended the practice of sending trustworthy persons from place to place to tax the people according to their means and to collect these taxes.[64] Pope Nicholas IV (1288–1292) urged the bishops to convoke synods to promote greater co-operation between the faithful and members of the Hospitallers and Knights Templars.[65] Representatives of these orders were to be received with hospitality in the diocese, and were to be permitted to work unmolested in behalf of the Holy Land. This latter provision no doubt included the collecting of alms.[66]

These instances indicate that the special needs created by the Crusades gave impetus to the practice of alms-gathering. They furnish furthermore an explanation why the enactments of the Church governing the collecting of alms have always been general, and have not been restricted to the mendicant orders. As will be seen later, this was true of all legislation up to and including the Council of Trent.

---

[63] Potthast, I, n. 922; cf. Epistola "*Gravis orientalis terrae*"—*MPL*, CCXIV, 828–832.

[64] Potthast, I, n. 4809.

[65] Two orders founded for and devoted primarily to the defense of the Holy Land. Cf. Fryar, "The Religious Military Orders"—*The Ecclesiastical Review* (originally, *The American Ecclesiastical Review*, Philadelphia, 1889–), XLVI (1912), 673–683. (Hereafter cited as *ER*.)

[66] Potthast, II, n. 23781 and n. 23783; cf. Schlee, *Die Päpste und die Kreuzzüge* (Halle, 1893), pp. 20–25.

CHAPTER II

MENDICANCY IN THE MENDICANT ORDERS

ARTICLE 1

PRACTICE OF EVANGELICAL POVERTY IN THE 11TH AND 12TH CENTURIES

The complete renunciation of private and common property, adopted by the mendicant orders of the thirteenth century, was not entirely an innovation. It was rather the result of many attempts to observe strictly the life practised by Christ and the apostles.[1]

The Church and the religious orders in the course of centuries acquired greater possessions, and with this increase of temporalities a proportionate relaxation of religious zeal and discipline set in. The Supreme Pontiffs, realizing the dangers which threatened the Church on numerous occasions, indicated the need of a return to a more exact observance of the teachings of Christ.[2]

As a consequence attempts at reform during the eleventh and twelfth centuries became numerous. The conceptions thus set forth as to the essence of apostolic Christianity varied widely. Their fundamental theme was the same. They insisted that spiritual men should live as Christ counselled.[3]

This will be evident from a brief survey of the reform movements of this period, both orthodox and heretical. Such a survey will also throw light on the reason for and the growth of mendicancy as practised in the following centuries among religious institutes.

[1] Schnürer, *Kirche und Kultur im Mittelalter* (2 vols., Paderborn: Ferdinand Schöningh, 1929), II, 330–332.

[2] Pierron, *Die katholischen Armen* (Freiburg im Breisgau, 1911), pp. 99–117; Ott, *Thomas von Aquin und das Mendikantentum*, p. 47.

[3] Davison, *Some Forerunners of St. Francis Assisi* (Boston and New York: Houghton, Mifflin Company, 1927), p. 31.

(*a*) *Monastic Reformers of the Eleventh and Twelfth Centuries*

The Carthusians were among the first to introduce poverty in its more severe form. The order was founded by St. Bruno (ca. 1032–1101) at Grenoble in the year 1084. St. Bruno desired for himself and his followers freedom from earthly possessions and temporal cares. To accomplish this ideal he insisted that the members of his institute should observe a very simple life. The institute, although its right to ownership was restircted to a minimum, did not in its early history collect alms. The order grew rapidly, for its severity appealed to many who like Bruno sought for holiness through renunciation of the world and worldly possessions.[4]

The Cistercians, founded by St. Robert of Molesme (ca. 1027-1111) in the year 1098, formed the second group to return to the primitive observance of evangelical poverty. The order in adopting the Rule of St. Benedict in its literal interpretation received official approbation from Pope Callistus II (1119–1124) in 1119.[5] The greatest austerity was prescribed. To eliminate every possibility of acquiring great wealth as the Benedictine monasteries had done, the Cistercians refused to avail themselves of the usual monastic source of revenue, without however renouncing ownership as an institute. The early history of the order furnishes no examples of members being sent out to collect alms for the necessities of life.[6]

Contemporary with the Carthusians and the Cistercians were the Good Men of Grammont, whose religious institute was founded by St. Stephen of Muret (1048–1124) in 1073. Poverty was most strictly observed. It became the objective ideal in the Rule which was written later and eventually was confirmed by

---

[4] Mabillon, *Annales Ordinis S. Benedicti* (ed. Lucca, 6 vols., 1739–1745), V, lib. XVI, 192; Davison, *Some Forerunners of St. Francis Assisi*, pp. 40–46.

[5] Jaffé, *Regesta Pontificum Romanorum ab condita Ecclesia ad annum post Christum natum MCXCVIII, ed. 2, correctam et auctam auspiciis Gulielmi Wattenbach curaverunt S. Loewenfeld, F. Kaltenbrunner, P. Ewald* (2 vols. in 1, Lipsiae, 1885–1888), I, n. 4969. (Hereafter cited as *Regesta Pontificum Romanorum.*)

[6] Mabillon, *Annales Ordinis S. Benedicti*, V, 87; Davison, *op. cit.*, pp. 69–72.

Pope Urban III (1185–1187) in 1186.[7] The Rule made many restrictions in regard to possessions. Begging was permitted only when there was no food in the house, and even then the local bishop was first to be informed of their state of need.[8]

Among the monastic reformers who attempted to restore pristine observance of evangelical poverty are to be numbered also the Premonstratensians founded by St. Norbert (ca. 1080–1134) in 1121. St. Norbert had at first no intention of establishing a new order, but endeavored to introduce reforms among the canons of St. Victor. He met with little success in this venture and, upon being asked to leave, withdrew to a deserted chapel on Mount Fürstenburg. From there he wandered through near-by villages, practising and preaching austerity of life. In this work he met with considerable success, and many followed his example. But he also stirred up antipathy on the part of ecclesiastics, and was accused at the Council of Fritzlar (1118) of assuming of his own accord the office of preaching, of dressing as a religious, and of retaining ownership of property. The Fathers of the Council upon hearing the evidence declared him innocent.[9]

Thereupon St. Norbert resigned his ecclesiastical preferments, disposed of his estate and gave the proceeds to the poor, reserving only what was necessary for the celebration of Holy Mass. Barefooted and begging he journeyed as far as St. Giles, where he met Pope Gelasius II (1118–1119), at whose request he retired to the solitude of Prémontré in the forest of Coucy. Disciples came to him in great numbers and he soon saw the necessity of adopting some definite form of life. He adopted the Augustinian Rule, but with some alteration provided for a far more rigid observance of poverty. However, in spite of the rigorous insistence on poverty, donations were invited with the proviso that the superfluous income be used for relieving the poor and unfortunate. When the order was definitely confirmed by Hono-

---

[7] Jaffé, *Regesta Pontificum Romanorum,* I, n. 1186.

[8] *Vita S. Stephani Grandimontensis, Regula,* cc. 12–14—*MPL,* CCIV, 1039–1041.

[9] Sess. IV—Mansi, XXI, 178.

rius II (1124–1130) in 1126, common ownership of property was granted.[10]

(*b*) *Heterodox Reformers*

The movement for the restoration of the primitive observance of poverty became so widespread that it found expression not merely in the establishment of new orders, but also in the rise of other associations, particularly lay organizations, many of which were later to be condemned.

One of the heretical sects of the eleventh and twelfth centuries which violently condemned the Church because of its temporal possessions were the Cathari, who were probably an offshoot of the early Manichean heresy. Southern France and northern Italy in particular became the hotbed of their activities. In these regions they were more commonly called Albigensians.[11]

In general, the Cathari and Albigensians denied most of the doctrines of the Church, and repudiated its hierarchy and ceremonies. They derided the Church especially by contrasting the worldliness of the Church's ministers with the simplicity of Christ and His disciples. They aroused popular enthusiasm through their own austere lives and by their preaching for the revival of the ideals and customs of the primitive Church.[12]

Other movements of a similar kind were begun by men like Peter of Bruys (+ ca. 1138), Henry of Lausanne (+ ca. 1145) and Arnold of Brescia (+ 1155), who likewise advocated the adoption of evangelical poverty. But these sects were short-lived, and were gradually amalgamated with the organization of the Waldenses, founded by a certain Peter Waldes (+ after 1179).

Peter Waldes, a rich merchant of Lyons, having heard the story of St. Alexius, was so deeply impressed that he determined

---

[10] Jaffé, *Regesta Pontificum Romanorum*, I, nn. 5232–5233; cf. Hugo, *Vie de St. Norbert* (Luxembourg, 1704), pp. 274–278; Davison, *Some Forerunners of St. Francis Assisi*, pp. 76–95.

[11] Felder, *The Ideals of St. Francis of Assisi*, p. 70; cf. Döllinger, *Sektengeschichte* (2 vols., München, 1890), I, 210–213; Davison, *Some Forerunners of St. Francis Assisi*, pp. 201–204.

[12] Moneta Cremonensis, *Adversus Catharos et Waldenses* (Romae, 1753), pp. 390–397; Felder, *The Ideals of St. Francis of Assisi*, pp. 70–71.

to divide his unearned riches among the poor and to adopt a life of extreme poverty and want.[13] Waldes, having disposed of his property, possessing neither gold nor silver, and relying on Divine Providence for his daily needs, commenced preaching to the people. His personality and his denunciation of the evils of the times attracted many followers. They also, following his example, sold their possessions and distributed them among the poor.

Many smaller groups joined the Waldenses, and before long their teachings were tainted with heretical tenets so that the Archbishop of Lyons insisted that their preaching be prohibited. In the III General Council of the Lateran (1179) Peter Waldes was summoned by Pope Alexander III (1159–1181) to appear before the assembled Fathers. Waldes was ordered to inform his followers that no preaching would be tolerated by ecclesiastical authorities unless the subject matter was first submitted for examination to members of the clergy.[14] For a time they heeded this admonition, but with the great increase in their numbers they reverted to their former practices and were officially condemned by Pope Lucius III (1181–1185) in 1181.[15]

The Waldenses made the practice of extreme poverty a prominent feature in their daily lives. They were divided into two groups, the *Perfecti* who devoted their time to the ministry, and the *Credentes* who remained at home, owned property and supported the *Perfecti* in their missions with the necessities of life.[16] Whenever the *Credentes* were not able to supply the necessary provisions they accepted alms and asked for them so that their brethren might be able to pursue their ministerial work unhampered. Mendicancy became a ready source of revenue for them,

[13] Pierron, *Die katholischen Armen*, p. 3; Müller, *Die Waldenser und ihre einzelnen Gruppen bis zum Anfang des 14ten Jahrhunderts* (Gotha, 1866), p. 4.

[14] Pierron, *loc. cit.*

[15] Decretum "*Ad abolendam*": ". . . In primis ergo Catharos, et Patarinos, et eos qui Humiliatos, vel Pauperes de Lugduno falso nomine mentiuntur, Passaginos, Josepinos, Arnoldistas, perpetuo decernimus anathemati subiacere."—Mansi, XXII, 476. The Waldenses were also called *Pauperes de Lugduno*. No definite date is assigned to the decree.

[16] Pierron, *op. cit.*, pp. 54–58.

as the rank and file of the people, edified by their austerity and hoping to share in the falsely assumed merit of their beneficiaries, gave willingly.[17]

Later the Waldenses divided into several groups. Some of them became reconciled with the Church and aided in counteracting the influences of the then powerful Albigensian sect. Pierron[18] enumerates three groups of reclaimed associations which had come under the influence of Peter Waldes: The *Humiliati Reconciliati* in 1201; the *Pauperes Catholici* in 1208; and the *Lombardi Reconciliati* in 1210.[19]

The Poor Catholics and the Reconciled Lombards soon began to disintegrate. Pope Innocent III (1198–1216) withdrew his encouragement and support in 1212, when he began to give his attention to the Preaching Friars of St. Dominic and the Friars Minor of St. Francis whose labors promised better results. On the other hand the *Humiliati* grew rapidly and became a strong bulwark within the Church in counteracting heresies.[20] Later, in the fifteenth and sixteenth centuries, the *Humiliati* became lax chiefly because of the accumulation of temporal goods and the reduction in their number. Pope Pius V (1566–1572) commissioned St. Charles Borromeo (1538–1584) to reform them. When a minority group threatened the death of St. Charles, the order was forthwith suppressed.[21]

Article 2

THE FRANCISCANS AND MENDICANCY

The movement towards the observance of evangelical poverty, up till then frequently tainted with heresy, was imbued with a true Christian spirit with the coming of St. Francis (1182–1226).

---

[17] Davison, *Some Forerunners of St. Francis Assisi*, pp. 268–269.

[18] *Die katholischen Armen*, pp. 54–58.

[19] Cf. Mann, *The Lives of the Popes in the Middle Ages* (18 vols., St. Louis: Herder Book Co., 1902–1932), XII, 272–275.

[20] Mann, *loc. cit.*

[21] Bulla *"Quemadmodum,"* 8 febr. 1571—*Bullarum Diplomatum et Privilegiorum Sanctorum Romanorum Pontificum Taurinensis Editio* (24 vols. et Appendix, Augustae Taurinorum, 1857–1872), VII, 885. Hereafter abbreviated and cited as *BRT*.

The reform which he introduced was in the tradition of Ss. Bruno (+ 1101), Norbert (+ 1134), and Bernard (1091–1153), and was accomplished with the approval of the Church. It aimed not at the destruction of traditional principles, customs, and institutions, but envisaged the repression of abuses and a return to the observance of evangelical poverty as practised by Christ and His apostles.[22]

(a) *St. Francis and Poverty*

St. Francis, like Waldes, the son of a rich merchant, began from early youth to cherish poverty and to consider it the basis for evangelical perfection. To him a life in the spirit of the Gospel was identical with a life of economic stability.[23] This manner of life he fully adopted on the 24th of February, 1209, after having heard at Portiuncula the Gospel narrative which describes the sending of the twelve apostles on their mission to evangelize the world: " Do not keep gold, or silver, or money in your girdles, no wallet for your journey, nor two tunics, nor sandals, nor staff; for the laborer deserves his living." [24] These words of the Gospel were a revelation embraced joyously by Francis: " That is what I seek, what I desire with all my heart." He cast away his staff and shoes, and exchanged his leather girdle for a rope, and his fine clothing for garments of coarse material.[25]

Bernard of Quintavalle (+ 1245), moved by a desire to give up all his possessions and to follow Christ in a life of poverty, became the first disciple of St. Francis. St. Francis invited him to the Church of St. Nicholas to discover from the Gospels what the Lord desired for them. The Book of Gospels was opened at three places selected by chance. The first text read: " If thou

---

[22] Dubois, *Saint Francis of Assisi, Social Reformer* (New York, Cincinnati, Chicago: Benziger Brothers, 1906), pp. 7–28.

[23] Felder, *The Ideals of St. Francis of Assisi,* p. 75.

[24] Matt. X, 9–10.

[25] Thomas de Celano, *S. Francisci Assisiensis vita et miracula* (edita curante Alenconiensis Eduardo, Romae, 1896), I, n. 16 and nn. 21–22. Thomas de Celano wrote two treatises of the life of St. Francis, the one in 1229 and the other in 1246. Hereafter the work of Celano will be cited as *Vita I* and *Vita II*. Cf. S. Bonaventura, *Legenda S. Francisci,* c. 3, n. 1—*Opera Omnia,* VIII, 510. (Hereafter cited as *Legenda S. Francisci.*)

wilt be perfect, go, sell what thou hast, and give to the poor." [26] In the second text they met the passage: " Take nothing for your journey, neither staff, nor wallet, nor bread, nor money: neither two tunics." [27] In the third the following passage was found: " If anyone wishes to come after me, let him deny himself, and take up his cross, and follow me." [28] " This is our life and rule," said the holy man of God, " and that of all who may join us. Go therefore, if you wish to be perfect, and do what you have heard." [29]

In the following year (1210), many new members having sought admission into his newly formed organization, Francis approached Innocent III and asked for approval of his society. The severity of the poverty which the founder inculcated caused Pope Innocent to hesitate in granting the apostolic approval.[30] This primitive Rule has not been recorded in history, although from the Testament of St. Francis it is evident that it consisted chiefly of Gospel texts to which were added several ordinances.[31] Thomas de Celano (ca. 1190—ca. 1260)[32] and St. Bonaventure (1221–1274)[33] expressed the view that the nucleus of the primitive Franciscan Rule was the observance of the Gospel literally after the manner which Christ prescribed for His apostles in sending them to evangelize the world.

These summary ordinances sufficed as long as the number of brothers remained limited. When candidates began to apply in greater numbers, the need of a revised Rule became obvious. Ac-

---

[26] Matt. XIX, 21.

[27] Luke IX, 3–4.

[28] Matt. XVI, 24.

[29] Thomas de Celano, *Vita I*, n. 28; S. Bonaventura, *Legenda S. Francisci*, c. 3, n. 3.

[30] Thomas de Celano, *Vita I*, nn. 32–34; Felder, *The Ideals of St. Francis of Assisi*, pp. 8, 11, 80–81; Sabatier, *Life of St. Francis* (New York, 1894), pp. 88–102.

[31] *Testamentum S. Patris Francisci:* ". . . Et ego paucis verbis et simpliciter feci scribi; et dominus papa confirmavit mihi."—*Opuscula Sancti Patris Francisci Assisiensis* (a PP. Collegii S. Bonaventurae, Ad Claras Aquas, 1904), p. 79.

[32] *Vita I*, n. 32.

[33] *Legenda S. Francisci*, c. 3, n. 8.

cordingly at a Chapter held in 1221 St. Francis proposed a new Rule which incorporated all the ordinances of earlier years with some additions to meet the needs of the rapid growth of the order.[84] This Rule, however, was soon supplanted by a much shorter one of twelve chapters in 1223. It was this Rule which received the formal approbation of the Holy See.[85]

In all three editions of the Rule of St. Francis poverty formed the nucleus of the Franciscan life, and his ideal of poverty may be briefly described as the "total renunciation of earthly things, and the greatest possible moderation in the use of these things."[86] In the Rule provision was made for members to obtain the necessities of life. St. Francis prescribed labor, and, if this did not suffice, they were to beg alms. But goods only, and not money, were to be accepted in either case.

The subsistence of the followers of Francis depended fundamentally upon alms, although he did stress labor as a means of livelihood. Obviously the brothers who remained in the monastery were dependent upon alms, since they received no revenue from their labor, and the monastery as such had no income from property. The Friars who were active with the apostolic ministry lived like St. Paul upon the voluntary offerings of the faithful. Whenever these did not suffice, they begged their daily sustenance from door to door.[87]

The first Rule limited the privilege of collecting alms to cases of necessity.[88] In the Rule of 1223 greater freedom was permitted in this matter. Rule II, Chapter VI, reads:

> The Friars shall appropriate nothing to themselves, neither a house nor place nor anything. And as pil-

[84] St. Francis wrote three Rules: the first, which Pope Innocent III confirmed without a bull, the second which Br. Elias lost, and the third, recorded and used today, which was confirmed by Pope Honorius III in 1223. Cf. *Opuscula Sancti Patris Francisci Assisiensis*, vii; Sabatier, "The Rule of 1221"—*The Life of St. Francis*, pp. 252–270.

[85] Honorius III, bulla "*Solet annuere,*" 29 nov. 1223—*Bullarium Franciscanum* (8 vols., Romae, 1759–1908), I, 15.

[86] Felder, *The Ideals of St. Francis of Assisi*, p. 94.

[87] Felder, *op. cit.*, p. 142.

[88] *Regula I*, c. IX, *De petenda eleemosyna—Opuscula Sancti Patris Francisci*, p. 37.

> grims and strangers in this world, serving the Lord in poverty and humility, let them go confidently for alms, nor should they be ashamed, because the Lord made Himself poor for us in this world. This is the sublimity of the highest poverty which has made you, my dearest brothers, heirs and kings of the kingdom of heaven: poor in goods but exalted in virtue.[39]

The change apparently resulted from the growth of the order, from the distribution of the work within the institute among a greater number of friars, and from the fact that the practice of working for people outside the community premises was gradually abandoned.

Indolence had no place in the Franciscan system. St. Francis was not slow in detecting the possibility of its infecting and corrupting the brethren. In his Testament he warned his disciples of the dangers of idleness. All were to be employed at some labor compatible with honesty, and only when the price of labor was not given were they to have recourse to the table of our Lord, begging alms from door to door.[40]

As already noted, money was definitely excluded in the quest of alms according to the ideals of St. Francis.[41] In his day money had already become a common medium of exchange, replacing the old system of trade and barter. St. Francis himself had witnessed the accumulation of wealth through money in the hands of a few, and the consequent increase of poverty among the masses.[42] He believed firmly in the brethren's literal observance of the injunctions of the Gospel: " Do not keep gold, or silver, nor money in your girdles." [43]

However difficult the observance of absolute poverty became with the growth of the order, St. Francis nevertheless considered it essential for the development of his original ideal. He main-

---

[39] Translation from *The Rule and General Constitutions of the Friars Minor* (Paterson, New Jersey: St. Anthony Guild Press, 1936), p. X.

[40] *Testamentum—Opuscula Sancti Patris Francisci*, p. 79.

[41] "Praecipio firmiter fratribus universis, ut nullo modo denarios vel pecuniam recipiant per se, vel per interpositam personam."—*Regula II*, c. IV—*Opuscula Sancti Patris Francisci*, p. 67.

[42] Felder, *The Ideals of St. Francis of Assisi*, pp. 120–121.

[43] Matt. X, 9.

tained that there existed between the world and the order an agreement that the order owed the world a good example, and the world in turn owed the friars a livelihood. He firmly believed that if the brethren remained true to poverty, salvation would come to the people among whom they lived, and that the people would therefore willingly support them. But in the degree in which the brethren abandoned poverty, in that degree the world would desert the brethren.[44]

(*b*) *Mitigations of the Rule of Poverty*

The first deviation from the strict observance of the Rule[45] came in connection with the care of churches, either given over to the custody of the order or actually erected by the friars. In the year 1229 the Chapter of St. James in Pisa donated a church to the friars,[46] and through apostolic requests other churches were handed over to the order. Thus, for instance, Gregory IX (1227–1241) explicitly asked bishops to entrust churches to them.[47] About the same time, and within a few years after the death of the holy founder, churches and monasteries were being constructed with apostolic approval by the friars themselves.[48]

The land necessary for these foundations was usually donated, and when this was not true it was provided by the Holy See, as was the case at Viterbo in 1236.[49] Material was needed for construction, and since the brethren did not own anything which

---

[44] "Quantum fratres declinabunt a paupertate, tantum mundus declinabit ab eis, et quaerent, inquit, et non invenient. Sed si Dominam meam Paupertatem complexi fuerint, mundus eos nutriet, quia mundo dati sunt ad salutem. Commercium est inter mundum et fratres: debent ipsi mundo bonum exemplum, debet eis mundus provisionem necessitatum."—Thomas de Celano, *Vita II*, n. 70.

[45] "Fratres nihil sibi approprient nec domum nec locum nec aliquam rem . . ."—*Regula II*, c. VI—*Opuscula Sancti Patris Francisci*, p. 68.

[46] *Bullarium Franciscanum*, I, 50 and I, 206.

[47] Const. "*Cum a nobis*," 9 febr. 1229—*Bullarium Franciscanum*, I, 48; cf. also I, 50 and I, 206.

[48] Gregorius IX, littera "*Recolentes*," 29 apr. 1228—*Bullarium Franciscanum*, I, 40; Gregorius IX, littera "*Ad audientiam*," 26 oct. 1232—*Bullarium Franciscanum*, I, 88.

[49] Gregorius IX, littera "*Religio vestra*, 9 dec. 1236—*Bullarium Franciscanum*, I, 209.

could be exchanged for such materials they had to depend upon alms. To insure the success of their collections, they frequently petitioned the Holy See to grant special favors to donors. Thus, in the erection of the church and monastery at Orvieto, Pope Gregory IX granted an indulgence of forty days to all who contributed for this purpose.[50]

Since the Rule forbade the friars to own anything, a question arose as to who were the true owners of these churches and monasteries. The question was submitted to Pope Gregory IX. He gave an official declaration and interpretation of the Rule of St. Francis in 1230, in which he indicated that title to all immovable property remained with the donors.[51] At the same time Pope Gregory IX attempted to settle the controversy about receiving money as alms. Donors, because of numerous requests and for the sake of convenience, preferred giving money in place of the actual objects which were needed. A "Syndic Apostolic" was to be appointed for every convent of the friars, who, acting in the name of the Holy See and of the donors, should administer, sell, or exchange all movable and immovable objects, and should also disburse the pecuniary alms and offerings for the necessities of the friars.[52]

During the reigns of Popes Innocent IV (1243–1254) and Alexander IV (1254–1261) privileges were readily granted, and mitigation of the pristine poverty became common. Pope Alexander IV permitted the friars to acquire in addition to their monasteries other property which they developed into gardens, although technically title to the property remained with the Holy See.[53]

---

[50] Littera "*Quoniam,*" 17 mart. 1240—*Bullarium Franciscanum,* I, 274.

[51] Const. "*Quo elongati,*" 28 sept. 1230—*Bullarium Franciscanum,* I, 68. Balthasar (*Geschichte des Armutsstreites im Franziskanerorden bis zum Konzil von Vienne* [Muenster, 1911], p. 34) considers the words of Gregory IX, "*salvo locorum et domorum domino illis, ad quos noscitur pertinere,*" difficult to interpret, since the construction of edifices was usually accomplished by numerous donations of the faithful.

[52] Cf. Kazenberger, *The Book of Life* (3. ed., Paterson, N. J., 1905), pp. 111-112.

[53] Cf. Balthasar, *Geschichte des Armutsstreites im Franziskanerorden bis zum Konzil von Vienne,* pp. 36–49.

When St. Bonaventure became minister general of the order in 1257, abuses, particularly in the manner of collecting alms, were numerous. Shortly after his election he sent a letter to all the provinces of the order, in which he urged the correction of this laxity, lamenting that the order had to some extent lost its pristine fervor.[54] He regretted that the friars were so much engaged in the construction of huge edifices, incautiously receiving money and storing it up, contrary to the spirit of St. Francis, and thereby arousing the curiosity of the faithful. Some were demanding too much hospitality while staying with friends. Others allowed themselves too much familiarity with the people of the world and gave no thought to curtailing their expenses as the vow of poverty demanded. He also warned that not infrequently superiors were negligent in controlling those who were entrusted with the office of collecting alms. However, in this same letter St. Bonaventure admitted that not all were guilty of this infidelity to the Rule.[55]

Moreover, St. Bonaventure was convinced that the order could not return to its pristine rigor. He believed in retaining the privileges already granted, and even in acquiring new ones if necessary. In his works he defended the necessity of studies, and the erection of large though not sumptuous edifices where the junior brothers could be educated and provided for.[56]

Henceforth the question of rigorous poverty was a continual issue in dispute. The Franciscans were divided into two groups, the Spirituals who believed in the strict observance of the Rule, and the Conventuals who favored a certain flexibility in the adaptation of the Rule to meet the needs created by the immense growth of the order.[57] Besides, there were not wanting those outside the order who condemned the Rule of St. Francis with its

---

[54] *Epistola I—Opera Omnia,* VIII, 468–469.

[55] ". . . licet autem plurimi reperiantur, qui non sunt culpabiles in aliquo praedictorum, tamen omnes involvit haec maledictio, nisi a non facientibus his qui faciunt, resistatur."—*Epistola I,* n. 3.

[56] Holzapfel, *Manuale Historiae Ordinis Fratrum Minorum* (Friburgi-Brisgoviae, 1909), pp. 30–35.

[57] Balthasar, *Geschichte des Armutsstreites im Franziskanerorden bis zum Konzil von Vienne,* pp. 155–169.

special stress on the vow of poverty. Pope Nicholas III (1277–1280) decided to intervene and issued a Bull, *Exiit qui seminat,* on the 14th of August, 1279.[58] He justified the Rule of St. Francis, and attempted to solve the misunderstandings relative to the interpretations which were dividing the order. He held that complete renunciation even of common property was meritorious and holy, since Christ confirmed it by word and example. The brethren were to live on alms either freely offered to them or humbly begged, or on what they might gain by the labor of their hands. Dominion or ownership was forbidden, but not the use of necessities.

The Bull of Pope Nicholas III, however, did not settle the disputes. The controversy continued and led up to the "*Magna Disputatio*" at Avignon in 1310–1312. Consequent upon this, Pope Clement V (1305–1314) issued a Constitution at the Council of Vienne (1313). In this Constitution, "*Exivi de paradiso,*"[59] the provisions of Nicholas III were reasserted; the renunciation of property was preserved, and the friars were allowed only the use of the goods given them.

Thereafter discussions on the issue arose between the Franciscans and the Dominicans themselves. This led to a complete reversal of ecclesiastical legislation on the vow of poverty by Pope John XIII (1316–1334).[60] According to this Constitution ownership of property was vested no longer in the Holy See, but in the order itself. However, on November 1, 1428, Pope Martin V (1417–1431) in a Constitution, "*Amabiles fructus,*"[61] permitted the Franciscans of the Observance to return to absolute poverty with complete renunciation of all temporal goods. In the following century the Council of Trent (1545–1563) decreed that in the future all monasteries, both of men and of women, even in the mendicant orders, could own real property (*bona immobilia*), with the exception that the Minor Observants and the Capuchins

[58] *Bullarium Franciscanum,* III, 440; this Bull is contained in the decretals, c. 3, *de verborum significatione,* V, 12, in VI°.

[59] C. 1, *de verborum significatione,* V, 11, in Clem.

[60] Const. "*Ad conditorem canonum,*" 8 dec. 1322—c. 3, *de verborum significatione,* tit. XIV, in Extrav. Ioan. XXII.

[61] *Bullarium Franciscanum,* VII, 712.

could continue in following the rule of absolute poverty as prescribed by St. Francis.[62]

Article 3

THE DOMINICANS AND MENDICANCY

A few years prior to the founding of the Franciscan order the foundations of the Dominican order were laid. St. Dominic, like St. Francis, loved poverty, not merely because of its ascetical value, but also because of the social vigor which accompanied it.[63]

St. Dominic did not immediately introduce renunciation of private and common property in establishing the order, but strove towards that end and accomplished the same by degrees. When the order was definitely approved by Pope Honorius III (1216–1217) in 1216,[64] it was allowed to retain title to ownership, although some authors hold that complete renunciation of property was the rule at the very time of pontifical approval.[65] It seems that the Church intended absolute poverty for the preachers. This was already indicated in a papal Bull of Pope Honorius III in 1219, in which he recommended the newly founded order to prelates of the entire Church.[66] In any event no doubt can be entertained that after the General Chapter which was held in the year 1220 at Bologna absolute renunciation of all property was

---

[62] Conc. Trident., sess. XXV, *de regularibus*, c. 3.

[63] Lambermond, *Der Armutsgedanke des hl. Dominikus und seines Ordens* (Zwolle, Holland: Verlag Waanders, 1926), p. 10. (Hereafter cited as *Der Armutsgedanke des hl. Dominikus.*)

[64] Bulla "Religiosam vitam," 22 dec. 1216—*Bullarium Ordinis Praedicatorum* (sub auspiciis SS. D.N.D. Benedicti XIII, 8 vols., Romae, 1729–1740), I, 2 (Hereafter cited as *Bull. Ord. Praed.*). Cf. also *BRT*, III, 309.

[65] Cf. Lambermond, *Der Armutsgedanke des hl. Dominikus*, pp. 11–13.

[66] Bulla "*Dilecti filii*," 8 dec. 1219: "Dilecti filii Prior et Fratres Ordinis Praedicatorum provide attendentes, quod, qui abscondunt frumenta, maledicuntur in populis, . . . seminant incessanter, et sarcinis divitiarum mundanarum abiectis, quo expeditius currant per mundi huius agrum, quem plus solito sentes operiunt vitiorum, in abjectione voluntariae paupertatis eunt, et flentes semina sua mittunt . . ."—*Bull. Ord. Praed.*, I, 8; cf. Balme-Lelaidier, *Cartulaire ou histoire diplomatique de St. Dominique* (2 vols., Paris, 1892), II, 368.

binding on the order.[67] Whether the decree of the Chapter included every possible form of renunciation has remained a matter of dispute. According to some authors this renunciation was not understood to include the convents in which the brethren actually lived.[68]

Upon the renunciation of private and common ownership some other source of revenue was needed to provide for the necessaries of life for the members of the order in their apostolic missions. Begging became necessary under the circumstances and it was welcomed by St. Dominic as a source of strength for his followers.[69] But they were to beg only for the needs of the day and no more. If there was a sufficiency in the monastery for the day, the brethren were not to be sent out to collect alms, nor were they to accept voluntary offerings that day.[70]

The question of refusing alms in money did not arise in the Dominican order. It cannot be proved from history that St. Dominic had any repugnance to the acceptance of money in the collecting of alms. He seems to have recognized that money was already a common medium of exchange, that it was far more practical in providing for the needs of the religious, and that it

---

[67] "Tunc etiam ordinatum est ne possessiones vel reditus de cetero tenerent fratres nostri . . ."—*Acta Capitulorum Generalium Ordinis Praedicatorum* (recensuit B. M. Reichert in *Monumenta Ordinis Praedicatorum Historia,* Tomus III, Romae, 1898–1899), I, 1 (Hereafter cited as *Acta Cap. Gen.*). Cf. Pierron, *Die katholischen Armen,* p. 139.

[68] Cf. Masetti, *Monumenta et Antiquitates Veteris Disciplinae Ordinis Praedicatorum ab Anno 1216–1348* (2 vols., Romae, 1864), I, 78, 80, 81, 87. A letter issued by Pope Innocent IV seems to indicate that this renunciation did not include the actual convents in which the brethren lived. The letter, "*Qui deum,*" 3 febr. 1244 reads: ". . . Cum humilitas vestra sibi de latitudine orbis terrae, nihil praeter domos et hortos, cum virgultis, praemiorum obtentu coelestium duxerit reservandum, Nos pie volentes, quod illorum fructus integrae vestrae paupertatis usibus applicentur, nullus a vobis decimas exigere vel extorquere praesumat auctoritate praesertim districtius inhibemus . . ."—*Analecta Sacri Ordinis Fratrum Praedicatorum seu Vetera Ordinis Monumenta Recentioraque Acta* (Romae, 1893–; ab anno 1907: *Analecta Sacri Ordinis Fratrum Praedicatorum*), III (1897–1898), 100.

[69] Quetif-Echard, *Scriptores Ordinis Praedicatorum* (Paris, 1719), I, 54.

[70] Quetif-Echard, *op. cit.,* I, 51; Lambermond, *Der Armutsgedanke des hl. Dominikus,* p. 24.

did not entail the inconveniences connected with gathering alms and commodities such as bread, corn, and other supplies in kind.[71]

The membership of the Dominican order grew rapidly. It was not long before definite regulations were required for governing the members in soliciting alms. Thus at the General Chapter held at Bologna in the year 1223 it was decreed that permission to go begging from house to house be not too readily granted.[72] The Chapters held at Paris in 1243 and at Bologna in 1244 issued regulations in regard to the territory in which the religious were to collect alms, but provided that they should not enter the territory of another province without the permission of the respective provincial.[73]

By the middle of the thirteenth century the order had encountered many difficulties in collecting the necessary alms. The collecting of alms had allured the poverty-stricken generally, and was practised by people who belonged to no religious institute. The faithful thus became impatient of appeals, and only reluctantly responded to them. The brothers to whom the office of begging was assigned reported this difficulty to their superiors, and frequently accepted this office only reluctantly.[74] The matter was submitted to the Chapter at Cologne in 1245, which insisted that the brothers were to collect alms in the territory in which they lived as a token of the poverty which they professed.[75]

Humbertus de Romanis (+ 1277), the fifth general of the order (1254–1263), carefully outlined the duties of the alms-gatherers, and the qualifications of the brothers to be charged with this responsibility. He established fixed rules for the activities of the questors in their association with others, particularly with women. When entering a house, a brother should not be alone, but should be accompanied by another. If money be given, it

---

[71] Lambermond, *op. cit.*, pp. 24–26.

[72] "Quod non detur de facili licentia fratres eundi de domo ad domum." —Reicherts, *Acta Cap. Gen.*, I, 4.

[73] Reichert, *Acta Cap. Gen.*, I, 26 and I, 29.

[74] Lambermond, *Der Armutsgedanke des hl. Dominikus*, p. 25.

[75] "Fratres in locis ubi habitant, panem petant in signum paupertatis."—Reichert, *Acta Cap. Gen.*, I, 32.

should be accepted and used for buying the necessities of life according to the direction of the superior.[76]

Despite the precautions thus taken, abuses in the collecting of alms arose also among the Dominicans, and complaints had been sent to Rome by bishops and archbishops shortly after the founding of the order. Pope Honorius III as early as 1221 asked bishops to punish members of the Order of Preachers who were guilty of abuses.[77] The General Chapter held at Paris in 1234 recognized these abuses and warned against them.[78]

In the course of time dependence on alms as the sole means of subsistence became increasingly difficult even in the Dominican Order. The rank and file looked forward to eventual ownership of property, despite the repeated interdicts of General and Provincial Chapters. Alms-gathering as the sole means of supporting a religious order failed for two reasons. First, the collecting of alms fell rapidly into disrepute; secondly, too many mendicant organizations had sprung up, and thus the source of income from alms was being tapped by too many claimants. The income thus became insufficient for the needs of the order, and lack of ownership threatened to imperil the realization of the very purpose of teaching and preaching.[79]

Partial ownership of common property was accordingly granted to the Dominicans in 1425 by Pope Martin V.[80] Finally, in 1475 the order petitioned Pope Sixtus IV (1471–1484) for the unrestricted right to hold common property. This right was granted by means of two papal constitutions, the first issued in 1475 and the second in 1477.[81]

---

[76] *De Vita Regulari* (edita curante Joachim Berthier, O.P., Romae, 1888–1889), II, 285.

[77] Littera "*Cum qui recipit,*" 4 febr. 1221—*Bull. Ord. Praed.*, I, 12.

[78] "Admonemus ne fratres impediant quaestuarios Sancti Antonii, sive alios, repellendo testimoniales litteras habentes, et modum generalis consilii observantes."—Reichert, *Acta Cap. Gen.*, I, 4.

[79] Cf. Lambermond, *Der Armutsgedanke des hl. Dominikus*, pp. 85–98; Turner, *The Vow of Poverty*, pp. 33–34.

[80] Const. "*Sincerae devotionis,*" 6 sept. 1425—*Bull. Ord. Praed.*, II, 654; const. "*Ecclesiarum,*" 21 nov. 1425—*Bull. Ord. Praed.*, II, 656.

[81] Const. "*Considerantes,*" 1 iul. 1475—*Bull. Ord. Praed.*, III, 528; const. "*Nuper per,*" 13 apr. 1477—*Bull. Ord. Praed.*, III, 550.

CHAPTER III

ALMS-GATHERING LEGISLATION BEFORE THE PROMULGATION OF THE CODE OF CANON LAW

The historical conspectus thus far given sheds light on the need for the development of legislative enactments of the Holy See to govern alms-gathering by religious. After the rise of the two great mendicant orders, the Franciscans and the Dominicans, there were approved by the Holy See other religious orders and religious institutes which either professed absolute poverty, or at least shared in the privileges of the mendicant orders. As early as the II General Council of Lyons (1274) the Hermits of St. Augustine and the Carmelites were reckoned among the four mendicant orders.[1] Later, in the fifteenth century, Pope Martin V approved the Servants of the Blessed Virgin Mary, whose institute usually has been listed in papal documents as fifth in the group of mendicant orders.[2]

Subsequently other religious institutes, particularly clerics regular, obtained from the Holy See in part or in whole the privileges of the mendicant orders. It is beyond the scope of this work to consider the historical development of mendicancy in each of the respective religious institutes. Such a study is not necessary to an understanding of the reason for and the development of legal enactments of the Church in governing alms-gathering by religious. It is therefore opportune at this point to pass to an examination of the general legislation of the Church in regard to alms-gathering.

Article 1

General Legislation Before the Council of Trent (1543–1565

The collecting of alms in general, as has been noted before, was

[1] Mansi, XXIV, 96.

[2] Confirmatio regulae "*Sedis Apostolicae,*" 16 mart. 1424—*BRT,* IV, 702–707.

practised from the very beginning to provide for the social needs of mankind. It played an important and useful rôle in the Church in providing for the support of the hierarchy, and of hospices and other charitable institutions.[3] However, the collecting of alms in the sense of going from place to place or from house to house was not practised to any great extent before the rise of the mendicant orders and the advent of the Crusades. It was then that the term *quaestores* came into use.

From this time on the permission to collect alms was readily granted and with few restrictions. Upon request the *quaestores* obtained the privilege of conceding indulgences and other favors to those who gave contributions. Abuses of all kinds soon crept in, particularly in the matter of publishing fabricated and fictitious indulgences.[4]

Pope Innocent III (1198–1216) in a letter to the Archbishop of Lyons severely condemned the abuses which were being practised in the quest of alms by the Hospitallers of St. John and by others who under the false pretext (*sub cruce falso signatos*) of being members of the order, collected in its behalf.[5] According to this letter certain individuals while collecting alms under this false pretext struck an assistant priest in a church and dared to celebrate Mass there before reconciliation had taken place. Then there were priests who, although suspended by their own bishops, had been presumptuously restored to their previous status by the Hospitallers. Thus falsely fortified they were sent, feigning to be religious, to collect alms in behalf of the order. The Pope ordered the Archbishop to inflict severe penalties throughout his province on all those who under a false pretext dared to continue collecting alms; lay people were to be excommunicated and clerics

---

[3] Mannucci, "De Historia Iuris Quaestuandi,"—*Analecta Ecclesiastica,* XVII (1909), 289, n. 6.

[4] Mostazo, *De Causis Piis* (Lugduni, 1668), lib. VII, c. XIII, n. 1.

[5] *Sub cruce falso signatos:* The brethren of the Hospitallers of St. John wore a cross on their monastic garb. Others who were not members of the order were sent to collect alms in the garb of the order to assure greater success.—Glossa ad c. 11, X, *de privilegiis et excessibus privilegiatorum,* V, 33, ad v. *signatos.*

suspended; and absolution from the censures was to be deferred until they refrained from these evil practices.[6]

The manner and method of collecting alms became an object of thorough discussion at the IV General Council of the Lateran in 1215.[7] Definite regulations were set up in canon 62 of the Council. Collecting of alms was henceforth to be entrusted to those only who had a letter of explicit permission from the Supreme Pontiff or from the diocesan bishop, and who were noted for their modesty and discretion. These regulations were held in high esteem and embodied in the Decretals of Gregory IX (1227–1241).[8] They formed the basis of future canonical legislation on the collecting of alms, particularly on the part of religious,[9] and therefore they are given here as found in the Decretals:

> Eleemosynarum quoque quaestores, quorum quidam, se alios mentiendo, abusiones nonnullas in sua praedicatione proponunt, nisi Apostolicas vel dioecesani Episcopi literas veras exhibeant prohibemus, et tunc praeter id, quod in ipsis continebitur literis, nihil populo proponere permittantur. Formam vero, quam communiter talibus Apostolica Sedes indulget, duximus exprimendam, ut secundum eam dioecesani Episcopi suas literas moderentur. Ea siquidem talis est: Quoniam, ut ait Apostolus, *omnes stabimus ante tribunal Christi, recepturi prout in corpore gessimus, sive bonum fuerit sive malum:* oportet nos diem messionis extremae misericordiae operibus praevenire, ac aeternorum intuitu seminare in terris, quod, reddente Domino, cum multiplicato fructu recolligere debeamus in coelis, firmam spem fiduciamque rectam tenentes, quoniam qui parce seminat parce et metet, et qui seminat in benedictionibus, et metet vitam aeternam. Quum igitur ad sustentationem Fratrum et egenorum

[6] ". . . Si quos clericos aut laicos a dictis fratribus (Hospitalis S. Ioannis) pro colligendis eleemosynis cruce falso signatos inveneris, his, a quibus ipsos missos constiterit, per totam provinciam tuam exhortationis officium interdicas; missos, si laici fuerint excommunicationis mucrone percellas, si clerici, ab officio beneficioque suspendas."—c. 11, X, *de privilegiis et excessibus privilegiatorum,* V, 33.

[7] Mansi, XXII, 1050.

[8] C. 14, X, *de poenitentiis et remissionibus,* V, 38.

[9] Mannucci, "De Historia Iuris Quaestuandi,"—*Analecta Ecclesiastica,* XVII (1909), 289, n. 7.

> ad tale confluentium hospitale propriae non suppetant facultates, universitatem vestram monemus et exhortamur in Domino, atque in remissionem vobis iniungimus peccatorum, quatenus de bonis vobis ad Deo conlatis pias eleemosynas et grata eis charitatis subsidia erogetis; ut per subventionem vestram ipsorum inopiae consulatur, et vos per haec bona et alia, quae Domino inspirante feceritis, ad aeterna possitis gaudia pervenire. Qui autem ad quaerendas eleemosynas destinantur modesti sunt et discreti, nec in tabernis aut in aliis locis incongruis hospitentur, nec inutiles facient aut sumptuosas expensas, caventes omnino, ne falsae Religionis habitum gestent.

Subsequent diocesan synods stressed the importance of the Lateran regulations, and frequently issued norms and decrees of their own to check the continuance of abuses. Already in the Synod of Narbonne in the year 1227 it was required that the decree of the Lateran Council concerning the collecting of alms be strictly adhered to. The synod further insisted that the *quaestores* be forbidden to preach in churches, and that they be allowed to read there only their papal or episcopal letters.[10]

The decree of the General Council was, however, generally ignored, and in consequence abuses became rampant. Even fictitious letters of the popes were forged. The diocesan synod at Trier (1227) attempted to remove this abuse by decreeing that no *quaestor* should collect alms in the diocese without the special permission of the bishop or of his *officialis,* and that whoever wantonly disregarded this ruling was to be publicly rebuked.[11]

The Synod of Mainz (1233) imposed further restrictions by forbidding *quaestores* to preach in any church or to display their relics publicly. Permission to collect alms was to be granted only for justifiable reasons, and the latter were to be examined by the bishop himself.[12] In the Synod of Montpellier (1258) a ruling was passed forbidding even a suffragan bishop to issue a letter of recommendation for the purpose of collecting alms wtihout

---

[10] Canon 6—Hefele, *Conciliengeschichte* (2. ed., 9 vols., Freiburg im Breisgau, 1873-1890), V, 894.

[11] Capitulum 6—Hefele, *Conciliengeschichte,* V, 950.

[12] Canons 29-30—Hefele, *op. cit.,* V, 1029.

first having obtained a special letter from the metropolitan.[13] At a subsequent Synod of Mainz (1261) renewed efforts were made to check the ever-growing abuses. Letters from the Pope, it seems, could no longer be relied upon, since in many instances the pastors were not able to identify the writing of the Supreme Pontiff. A solution was sought by renewing the decree that a letter of permission granted by the bishop himself be required. When the *quaestores* made their appearance, the pastors were diligently to explain to the faithful the reasons why alms were to be collected in the parish.[14] In its forty-eighth canon the synod ordained that the Brothers of St. Anthony were to be given permission to collect alms but once a year. This collection was to be taken up by the brothers themselves, and not by others. When they came, the pastors were to announce the nature and purpose of the collection.

However, the general legislation of the Church as well as the particular decrees enacted in diocesan synods did not offer the necessary safeguards in the constantly multiplying difficulties which ecclesiastical superiors encountered with the *quaestores*. The practice of collecting alms increased everywhere. Not merely religious but also lay organizations formed guilds during the thirteenth and fourteenth centuries to collect alms chiefly as a means of livelihood.[15] Lies concerning indulgences, relics and other objects were devised to induce the faithful to give alms more readily, so much so that the preaching of indulgences and the display of relics became occasions from which great scandal in the Church frequently arose.[16]

The glaring excesses in the collecting of alms were enumerated in the Council of Vienne (1311–1312):

> It has been brought to our attention that some of these *quaestores* of their own accord, with daring temerity and with great misleading of souls, grant indulgences to the people, dispense from vows, absolve those

[13] Canon 8—Hefele, *op. cit.*, V, 1029.

[14] Canon 17—Hefele, *op. cit.*, VI, 70.

[15] Hostiensis, *Commentaria in quinque libros decretalium* (5 vols., in 3, Venetiis, 1581), ad c. 14, X, *de poenitentiis*, V, 38.

[16] Mostazo, *De Causis Piis*, lib. VII, c. XIII, n. 1.

> who confess to them from perjury, from homicide and from other sins, upon receiving a certain amount of money declare them free from paying back stolen goods, release them from a third or a fourth of the penance enjoined upon them, and (as they falsely assert) draw from purgatory three or more souls of parents and friends to lead them to celestial happiness; they grant to benefactors who reside in their territories a plenary remission of sins, and (to use their words) absolve them from every punishment and fault.[17]

Pope Clement V (1305–1314) vehemently condemned the excesses, and, in order to preclude any recurrence of the abuses, withdrew all the privileges which were in any way granted to orders or individual persons. In the aforementioned Council he ordained that the Apostolic letters were to be carefully examined by the bishops themselves, who were to watch diligently in the future that the *quaestores* would not grant any indulgences beyond those authorized in the Apostolic letters, and that the soliciting of alms be done in all simplicity and modesty. Henceforth their preaching was to be restricted to an explanation of the letters, and any violation in this matter was to be punished with ecclesiastical penalties and censures.[18]

These regulations of the Council of Vienne, though stringent, met with comparatively little success, as will be seen in the following article.

Article 2

LEGISLATION OF AND AFTER THE COUNCIL OF TRENT

(*a*) *Legislation in General*

The Fathers of the Church at the Council of Trent (1543–1565) were fully cognizant of the many difficulties which the Church had encountered with the *quaestores*. The remedies prescribed in previous Councils and in papal constitutions had to a great extent failed, and the scandal and complaints of the faithful seemed rather to increase. Two decrees therefore were issued

---

[17] C. 2, *de poenitentiis et remissionibus,* V, IX, in Clem. Translation by the writer.

[18] C. 2, *de poenitentiis et remissionibus,* V, IX, in Clem.

by the Council, one in the fifth session and the other in the twenty-first session.

The former of these decrees forbade *quaestores* to preach either personally or through others. Those who dared to violate this injunction were to be punished by bishops and local Ordinaries with suitable penalties, notwithstanding any previous privileges to the contrary.[19]

The other decree of the Council aimed at abolishing entirely the office of *quaestores,* regardless of the privileges formerly granted to churches, to monasteries, to hospitals, to pious places, and to all persons of any and every rank, condition and dignity whatsoever, and notwithstanding immemorial customs.[20]

The decree of the Council of Trent in nowise settled the problem, for by abolishing the office of *quaestor,* it made no provision for the need of relief on account of which the office of *quaestor* was originally instituted. The need of relief was still there. Some substitute was still demanded for the Peter's Pence collection, the collection for the Holy Land entrusted to the Friars Minor of the Observance, and the collections for charitable institutions. Besides, there were still mendicant orders which themselves possessed no communal property.[21]

The decrees of the Council of Trent apparently touched all the religious institutes. Consequently attempts were made to deny also to mendicant orders the privilege of collecting alms. Pope St. Pius V (1566–1572) realized the hardships which would result, particularly for the mendicant orders, from the strict ob-

---

[19] "Quaestores vero eleemosynarii, qui etiam quaestuarii vulgo dicuntur, cuiuscumque conditionis existant, nullo modo per se, nec per alium praedicare praesumant: et contra facientes ab episcopis et ordinariis locorum, privilegiis non obstantibus, opportunis remediis omnino arceantur."—sess. V, *de ref.,* c. 2, in fine.

[20] ". . . ut posthac quibuscumque christianae religionis locis eorum [quaestorum eleemosynarum] nomen atque usus penitus aboleatur, nec ad officium huiusmodi exercendum ullatenus admittantur: non obstantibus privilegiis ecclesiis, monasteriis, hospitalibus, piis locis, et quibusvis cuiuscumque gradus, status, et dignitatis personis, concessis, aut consuetudinibus etiam immemorabilibus."—sess. XXI, *de ref.,* c. 9.

[21] Mannucci, "De Historia Iuris Quaestuandi,"—*Analecta Ecclesiastica,* XVII (1909), 289, n. 8.

servance of the decree. In his Constitution "*Etsi mendicantium*" of May 16, 1567, the decrees of the Council were given a benign interpretation. Pope Pius declared that the legislation of the Church did not apply to the mendicants, since their very existence depended upon the right to collect alms. Hence they were to be permitted to collect them.[22]

Even this Constitution of Pope St. Pius V did not settle the matter. The Sacred Congregation of the Council therefore on June 12, 1608, issued the following interpretation: The Sacred Congregation of Cardinals, interpreters of the Council of Trent, declare that the mendicants are in nowise forbidden to collect alms, provided, however, that others be not in any way authorized to collect in their name.[23]

Gradually the collecting of alms was again generally resumed. Collections were taken up for monasteries, hospitals and other pious institutes, and the practice was not explicitly condemned by the Holy See. Indeed, Benedict XIV (1740–1758) recognized these collections as new methods, classifying those who collected alms as *collectarii,* and not as *quaestores,* which latter name the Council of Trent had condemned. The *collectarii,* although not immune from the excesses which had been practised by the *quaestores,* were thus reckoned as an entirely different group by Benedict XIV.[24]

After the granting of this recognition by the supreme authority rescripts for the collecting of alms were commonly issued by the Holy See to bishops. These rescripts ordained that only those be permitted to collect alms who in the judgment of the bishops were noted for their honesty and integrity of life. They were to collect alms not as if these were owed as debts, but in all simplicity and modesty. The *collectarii* were to be cautioned not to publish indulgences, not to preach, not to carry relics, nor in any way to induce the faithful to contribute by means of threats

[22] § 2, n. 15—*Codicis Iuris Canonici Fontes cura Emi Petri Card. Gasparri editi* (9 vols., Romae [later Civitate Vaticana] : Typis Polyglottis Vaticanis, 1923–1939. Vols. VII–IX ed. cura et studio Emi Iustiniani Card. Seredi), n. 121. Hereafter cited as *Fontes.*

[23] *Fontes,* n. 1643.

[24] Const. "*Quamvis iusto,*" 30 apr. 1749, §§ 9–10—*Fontes,* n. 398.

or imprecations. Above all, they were to go under the title *collectarii,* and not under the title *quaestores.*[25]

Giraldus (1692–1775) reports in his work, "*Expositio Iuris Pontificii,*"[26] a sample of a papal rescript based upon the decree of Pope Urban VIII (1623–1644) of July 12, 1644,[27] in which the Holy See cautions against abuses which had been practised before the Council of Trent, and in which the Holy See stipulated the precaution to be taken to preclude the possibility of a recurrence of such abuses. This rescript, granted to the Archconfraternity of the Holy Ghost of the Kingdom of Naples, reads as follows:[28]

> The Holy Father upon the opinion of the eminent cardinals, interpreters of the Council of Trent, grants the Archconfraternity of the Holy Ghost of the Kingdom of Naples at Rome the privilege of seeking alms for a period of five years under the title of the pious works which it claims to perform; with the proviso, however, that alms cannot be collected unless the permission of the ordinary of each of the Kingdom's dioceses in which they wish to collect be obtained in writing; and this is to be granted gratuitously. The persons deputed shall be furnished by the superiors of the said Archconfraternity with testimonial letters. These persons shall not be transients (*vagi*) or persons without an established domicile in the place of collection, but such as are well known there by name for their honesty, integrity, and piety. They shall not be of the number of those who are commonly called *quaestores,* and shall never exercise an office like theirs. They shall be called *collectarii,* and not *quaestores,* a title which the Council of Trent condemned. They shall not have a share in the alms collected, which shall be converted into the use of the mentioned pious works,

[25] Barbosa, *Collectanea Doctorum in Concilium Tridentinum* (Lugduni, 1672), sess. XI, *de ref.,* IX, ad n. 20.

[26] (2 vols., Romae, 1829), II, sect. 41 ad sess. XXI, *de ref.,* c. 9.

[27] This decree of Pope Urban VIII is cited by Pope Benedict XIV in his Constitution "*Quamvis iusto,*" 30 apr. 1749, § 10—*Fontes,* n. 398. According to this Constitution the decree itself may be found in the *Decreta Congregationis Concilii Tridentini,* lib. XVII, 350. The writer was not able to find the decree in sources available.

[28] Translated by the writer.

> but they shall have a sufficient and honest reward set aside for them. Let them perform their duties without any appearance of deceit or any manifestation of unreserve. They shall not carry with them any images, diplomas, briefs, relics or other similar things for arousing the emotions of the faithful, nor any other insignia or paraphernalia. They shall not make any signs or blessings over animals. They shall not preach or publish indulgences either themselves or through others; they shall not exhibit a list of privileges, even though such have been granted by the Holy See; they shall not offer Masses or other forms of prayer for the extorting of money or other goods; they shall not accept anything as due them in virtue of some vague custom or of some alleged contract executed by fraud; they shall not promise the prayers and intercessions of some popular saint in exchange for any benefactions received or receivable. Let them seek alms from the faithful in all simplicity and modesty, careful to forestall all occasion of scandal. If they belong to any regular order, they must be selected from the professed of the same order. They must use honest methods, receiving only that which is offered spontaneously and nothing beyond that. They shall not call a meeting even for the benefit of that Archconfraternity or pious work for which the alms are being collected. Before they are permitted to collect alms, they shall swear in the presence of the bishop or vicar general that they will faithfully observe the above-mentioned conditions. That these conditions may be observed let the bishops and the vicars general inquire not only through others, but even make it their own personal duty and obligation to inquire whether any fraud, and especially whether any contravention of the aforementioned conditions be committed. If any collectors shall be found guilty, let the authorities punish them publicly according to their own judgment and in proportion to the gravity of the fault, and remove them immediately from the office of collecting alms, regardless of whatever privileges they may possess, notwithstanding the confirmation of the Holy See or of immemorial custom.

The bishops based the formulary of their letters upon the formulation employed in papal rescripts when they permitted the *collectarii* to exercise their office. The letters usually demanded that whatever was collected be used exclusively for the purposes indicated, and that the *collectarii* proceed in all due modesty and without fraud, carefully shunning all means of extorting alms, which practice the Holy See so severely condemned.[29]

The Council of Trent, then, definitely abolished the term *quaestores.* Through a benign interpretation of its decrees the collecting of alms was again permitted, first to the mendicant orders, and later, under certain precautions, to other religious institutes which were promoting works of piety and did not have sufficient income of their own.[30]

Bishops were at first reluctant to permit the collecting of alms, but later granted the required permission, provided that the following points, copied from conditions in Apostolic letters, were verified: (1) that those who were designated to collect alms should be persons of respectable character, and should not be called *quaestores;* (2) that they should not be partakers of the alms collected, and that whatever compensation was necessary should be paid by a determined and adequate salary; (3) that they should not proclaim indulgences, carry relics, or exceed their privileges; (4) that they should not extort alms by embarrassing the people or by using threatening arguments; (5) that they should not carry bells or similar insignia; (6) that they should not insist that alms be paid them as though owed, or in

[29] Monacelli (1715) in his work, *Formularium Legale Practicum* (4 vols., Venetiis, 1736), I, tit. VI, cites a sample of an episcopal letter permitting an alms-gatherer to collect alms. It reads: "N. Epus. N. Ut tu qui honestae vitae, probataeque pietatis exsistis, et ab officialibus . . . N. in quo hospitalitatis officium exercetur, deputatus fuisti, cum ad sustentationem confluentium peregrinorum (vel infirmorum) propriae non suppetant facultates (vel attentis piis operibus quae dicta sodalitas exercet, quorum manutentioni et adimplemento propriae non suppetunt facultates, et aliunde succurri non valet) eleemosynas, et grata charitatis subsidia per totam nostram dioecesim, modeste, et sine fraude, et dummodo indulgentias non publices, imagines sacras seu reliquias non circumferas, aliove improbo modo non extorqueas: nec de illis ullo modo participes, sed in usum dictorum piorum operum integre convertantur (de quo nobis officiales in visitatione et extra constare facient) perquirere et colligere valeas, licentiam ad . . . duraturam, gratis concedimus."

[30] Mostazo, *De Causis Piis,* lib. VII, c. XIII, nn. 10–11.

virtue of some claim sanctioned by custom, or in alleged fulfillment of a duty arising from a contract fraudulently extorted, or in consideration of prayers to be said by the donors; (7) that they should collect alms in forthright simplicity and chastened restraint.[31]

(*b*) *Legislation in Particular*

In the centuries following the Council of Trent extensive privileges in regard to the collecting of alms were granted to the mendicant orders and to other religious institutes through papal constitutions and by means of approval for the Constitutions of religious institutes. The term "mendicant" was generally applied to orders and congregations which by the terms of their original foundation were not entitled to ownership of property which would yield them regular sustenance.[32] In the strict sense only the Capuchins and the Friars Minor retained their original status of mendicancy,[33] and consequently they continued to depend upon extraneous sources for their means of support. The privilege of collecting alms when granted to other orders and congregations, which were classified as non-mendicant, was far more restrictive than theirs, as will be noted later.

1. Privileges of the Mendicant Orders

The privilege of the mendicant orders to collect alms without the permission of the local Ordinary in those places where their houses were situated was definitely established by a number of responses from the Sacred Congregation of Bishops and Regulars.[34] This privilege of the mendicant orders was also confirmed

[31] Barbosa, *Iuris Ecclesiastici Universi Libri Tres*, lib. I, c. 7, n. 78.

[32] "Members of Religious Orders Collecting Funds,"—*ER*, XL (1908), 414.

[33] Conc. Trident., sess. XXV, *de regularibus*, c. 3; cf. PCI, 16 oct. 1919—*AAS*, XI (1919), 478.

[34] S.C. Ep. et Reg. decr.: *Episcopo Casalensi*, 6 oct. 1597; *Collectori Portugalliae*, 2 aug. 1594; *in Ostunensi*, 15 febr. 1577; *in Papiensi*, 22 aug. 1581, et 3 dec. 1612; *in una Observantium*, 17 nov. 1620; *in una Cappuccinorum*, 5 oct. 1646—Ferraris, *Prompta Bibliotheca Canonica, Iuridica, Moralis, Theologica, necnon Ascetica, Polemica, Rubriscistica, Historica* (11 vols., Venetiis, 1782–1794), s.v. "Eleemosyna," n. 35 (Hereafter cited

by a special constitution of Pope Clement XI (1700–1721), "*Exponi nobis,*" of July 8, 1717.[35] It was based fundamentally upon the contention that bishops in granting permission for the establishment of a mendicant convent *ipso facto* consented to that convent's right of collecting alms in the future to provide for the needs of the institute.[36]

If alms were collected outside the place where the monastery or convent was situated, yet within the diocese, then the collectors were required to present to the bishop a testimonial letter of the religious superior. But no written permission of the bishop was required.[37]

In order that the mendicant orders might enjoy the abovementioned privilege, they were obliged to collect the alms themselves. If the alms were to be taken up by other religious or by seculars, then the explicit permission of the bishop was required.[38] Likewise, whenever collections were taken up outside their own diocese, then the mendicants, even though they personally undertook the office, were required to seek the permission of the Ordinary of the diocese where they intended to collect.[39]

---

as *Prompta Bibliotheca*). Cf. Piatus Montensis, *Praelectiones Iuris Regularis,* II, 47. These decrees are not listed in Bizzarri, or in any other source available to the writer.

[35] *BRT*, XXI, 763.

[36] "Non tenentur Regulares, qui ex institutione aut facultate Sedis Apostolicae eleemosynas quaeritare aut mendicare possunt, petere ab Ordinario licentiam eleemosynas per dioecesim quaerendi, cum in erectione Monasteriorum haec licentia eis tacite ab Ordnariis impertita censeature."—S.C. Ep. et Reg., 6 oct. 1597—Ferraris, *Prompta Bibliotheca,* s.v. "Eleemosyna," n. 35.

[37] S.C. Ep. et Reg., 25 maii 1703—Bizzarri, *Collectanea in usum Secretariae Sacrae Congregationis Episcoporum et Regularium* (Romae, 1885), p. 285 (Hereafter cited as Bizzarri). Cf. Fagnanus, *Ius Canonicum seu Commentaria Absolutissima in Decretalium Libros* (3 vols., Venetiis, 1764), ad c. 11, X, *de privilegiis,* V, 33, n. 3; Piatus Montensis, *Praelectiones Iuris Regularis,* II, 37.

[38] S.C.C., decr. *in Polianensi,* 24 sept. 1622; S. C. Ep. et Reg., decr. *in Mondulpho,* 17 ian. 1692; S.C.C., decr. *in Theanen.,* 30 apr. 1678—Ferraris, *Prompta Bibliotheca,* s.v. "Eleemosyna," nn. 38–39.

[39] Ferraris, *op. cit.,* s.v. "Eleemosyna," n. 35; Piatus Montensis, *Praelectiones Iuris Regularis,* II, 37.

2. Bishops and the Mendicants

Bishops were not permitted to prevent the mendicants who had houses established in their diocese from collecting alms, as long as they undertook the office themselves and adhered to the apostolic grants.[40] Nor could they raise objections on the score that several mendicant houses existed in the diocese, or that mendicants of different houses were collecting at the same time.[41]

Formerly severe penalties were decreed against bishops and others who forbade the mendicants to collect alms. These penalties, although now abrogated, threatened bishops with the interdict *ab ingressu ecclesiae,* and suspension from the government and administration of their churches, and those inferior to Ordinaries with excommunication.[42]

It was disputed among theologians and canonists whether bishops could prevent superfluous and immoderate collecting of alms on the part of those who possessed this privilege. Some held the affirmative view by contending that the bishop, as pastor of the diocese, was acting within his rights in checking abuses. Others, on the other hand, denied the bishop any authority in this matter. They maintained the view that bishops were to report abuses to the proper religious superiors. If this did not effect a satisfactory solution, then recourse could be had to the Holy See.[43]

Nevertheless, it seems undeniable that local Ordinaries did enjoy certain rights as local guardians of faith and morals. If a mendicant committed some public transgression or caused a public disturbance, the bishop could command him to return to his monastery, and the superior had to punish the delinquent with

---

[40] Urbanus VIII, const. "*Cum sicut,*" 9 febr. 1640—*BRT,* XV, 53.

[41] "Sacra Congregatio etc. censuit fratres Carmelitas discalceatos non esse molestandos, neque impediri posse in quaestuatione eleemosynarum, non obstante quod alii fratres mendicantes eadem die eleemosynas soleant quaestuare, et ita decrevit, et ab omnibus Regularibus mendicantibus et praesertim a fratribus S. Francisci de' Observantia observari mandat."—S.C. Ep. et Reg., *Carmelitarum,* 9 ian. 1608—*Fontes,* n. 1643.

[42] Sixtus IV, const. "*Sacri,*" 22 iul. 1479, § 8—*BRT,* V, 280; Ferraris, *Prompta Bibliotheca,* s.v. "Quaestuarii," n. 17; Piatus Montensis, *Praelectiones Iuris Regularis,* II, 37.

[43] Cf. Piatus Montensis, *Praelectiones Iuris Regularis,* II, 37–38.

proportionate penalties within a stated time. In case the superior failed in his duty, the bishop could then proceed himself.[44]

Furthermore, Pope Gregory XIV (1590–1591) in a constitution, "*Reminiscimur,*" of May 24, 1591, gave bishops certain rights when he forbade preachers to exhort the people to give alms without first consulting the bishop in the matter. This regulation apparently also included the mendicants whenever they were assigned the office of preaching to the people. If the regulars evaded this injunction, they were to be rebuked and punished by the bishop according to the gravity of their fault. However, Pope Gregory also warned the bishops to permit the regulars to collect alms in places where they were accustomed to preach at least once a year, under the proviso however that their monastery was really in need.[45]

3. Non-Mendicant Orders and Congregations

Greater supervision could be exercised by local Ordinaries with regard to non-mendicants. They were not permitted to collect alms, not even in the diocese where their monastery was situated, without the explicit permission of the Holy See or at least that of the local Ordinary; and in the latter instance they were required to abide by his instructions. The need of a special permission from the bishop was especially mandatory on members of diocesan institutes.[46] Greater detailed legislation for non-mendicant orders and congregations will be noted in the subsequent article.

4. Women Religious with Solemn Vows

The Holy See would not permit women religious with solemn

[44] Conc. Trident., sess. XXV, *de regularibus,* c. 14; S.C. Ep. et Reg. decreta: *In Spoletana,* 16 sept. 1596, 18 dec. 1600, et 3 dec. 1601; *In Lancianen.,* 5 febr. 1602 et 5 mart. 1602; *In Pistorien.,* 7 iun. 1602—Ferraris, *Prompta Bibliotheca,* s.v. "Quaestuarii," n. 9; cf. Heiner, "Das Kollektieren seitens der Ordensleute,"—*Archiv für katholisches Kirchenrecht* (Innsbruck, 1857–1861; Mainz, 1862–), XCI (1911), 100 (Hereafter cited as *AKKR*).

[45] *BRT,* IX, 428.

[46] S.C. Ep. et Reg. responsum (Anagnino Episcopo), 20 ian. 1769. This response is listed in *AKKR,* XCI (1911), 100. It is not listed in the *Fontes* or in Bizzarri's collection.

vows personally to collect alms. They were strictly obliged to observe the law of enclosure.[47] One of the reasons for the failure of the nuns to observe the law of enclosure was the poverty which forced them to go out begging for their subsistence.[48]

Pope St. Pius V in a constitution, "*Decori*," of February 1, 1570, ordained that extern sisters, who were not permitted to enter the cloister, be commissioned to collect alms for the nuns of monasteries which were in want. If this plan did not suffice, he left it to the discretion of the bishops to provide for the needs of the nuns in a suitable manner.[49]

Pope Gregory XIII (1572–1585), in his Constitution "*Deo sacris*," of December 30, 1572, likewise insisted on the observance of the enclosure of nuns, and issued instructions to provide for their necessities. All expenses were to be curtailed, even in those things which were useful and necessary. If this did not suffice, he ordained that the bishop of the diocese where the convent was situated was to select trustworthy men to gather alms in their behalf; relatives of the nuns, and the local laity generally, were to be informed of their needs, and petitions could be made through periodicals as long as the convent for which alms were sought was not mentioned by name. If these measures proved inadequate, the papal constitution demanded that the dowry required of the nuns be increased, and, as a last resort, that the nuns be sent to another monastery.[50]

5. Civil Interference in Alms-Gathering

On more than one occasion the Holy See stated that civil rulers lacked all jurisdiction in designating clerics and religious to collect alms.[51] But to what extent civil authorities could proceed

[47] Conc. Trident., sess. XXV, *de regularibus*, c. 3.

[48] Pennacchi, *Commentaria in Constitutionem Apostolicae Sedis* (2 vols., Romae, 1910), I, 706; Schaaf, *The Cloister* (The Catholic University of America Canon Law Studies, no. 13, Washington: The Catholic University of America, 1921), pp. 48–49.

[49] *Fontes*, n. 133.

[50] *BRT*, VIII, 30.

[51] S.C.C., *in Regiensi*, 9 ian. 1582; S.C.C., *in Aversana*, 22 febr. 1620; S.C. Ep. et Reg., *in Papiensi*, 8 nov. 1619—Ferraris, *Prompta Bibliotheca*, s.v. "Eleemosyna," n. 40.

against those who enjoyed the *privilegium fori* was a matter of dispute among authors. Mostazo, a canonist of the seventeenth century, discusses the opinions which various authors had on civil interference.[52] They may be classified into three groups.

The first group of authors denied civil authorities any right whatsoever, on the commonly accepted supposition that a civil officer or judge in respect to an ecclesiastical person is only a private person and consequently lacks jurisdiction.[53] The second group of authors maintained that if collectors were guilty of excesses they could be apprehended by a lay judge and returned to their respective superiors for punishment. This procedure they considered permissible and even necessary as a matter of defense to forestall future violations and to make possible the apprehension of such collectors by their superiors. These authors sanctioned this civil interference particularly in cases wherein clerics and religious collected alms under false pretenses.[54]

The third group of authors, whose opinion Mostazo favored, adopted the view of the second group, but with certain limitations. Ordinarily excesses were to be reported to the proper ecclesiastical authorities, who then were to proceed to the punishing of the culprits. Civil apprehension was permitted when public misdemeanors were perpetrated which could not be checked otherwise, and when the common social good demanded that action be taken. Such collectors could be seized and sent back to their superiors. Full authority was to be exercised in instances in which collectors of alms feigned to be in sacred orders, or dressed in a religious garb, when in reality they did not belong to any religious institute.[55]

Article 3

THE DECREES, "SINGULARI QUIDEM" OF MARCH 27, 1896, AND "DE ELEEMOSYNIS COLLIGENDIS" OF NOVEMBER 21, 1908

(a) *The Decree "Singulari quidem" of March 27, 1896*[56]

With the ever increasing duty of caring for the needs of charity

[52] *De Causis Piis*, lib. VII, c. XIII, nn. 5–9. The authors cited by Mostazo are not available to the writer.

[53] Mostazo, *ibid.*, n. 6.

[54] Mostazo, *loc. cit.*

[55] Mostazo, *ibid.*, nn. 7–9.

[56] *ASS*, XXVIII (1895–1896), 555–558; *Fontes*, n. 2029.

devolving upon the religious institutes of women, the collecting of alms by sisters in simple vows became more necessary and widespread. Formerly the sisters were wont to restrict the quest of alms to the localities where their convents were situated, but in the course of time they began to collect not only throughout the diocese itself, but also through neighboring dioceses, and in fact anywhere. Frequently the sisters were young and absented themselves from their conventual life for months at a time, and thus exposed themselves to many spiritual and physical dangers. Occasionally it happened that secular women dressed in religious garb went about the country soliciting alms.[57]

The Sacred Congregation of Bishops and Regulars in the introduction of the decree "*Singulari quidem*" expressed its recognition of the necessity of sending out women religious to solicit for charitable purposes, yet at the same time it stated its desire to check the dangers which could and did arise from promiscuous mendicancy. Many bishops had petitioned the Holy See to issue norms regulating the quest of alms by women religious. Upon mature and diligent deliberation definite regulations were formulated by the Sacred Congregation and embodied in this decree. They form a basis for the interpretation of the sacred canons governing the collecting of alms by women religious, and prescribe the method to be followed and the discipline to be observed by those who are selected for this mission.[58]

The provisions of this decree are summarized as follows:

1. Sisters in institutes with simple vows shall not collect alms except with the written permission of their own local Ordinary. If they wish to collect in another diocese they must obtain the additional permission of that local Ordinary.

2. The local Ordinary shall not grant this permission unless he is assured that there is real need, and that in his judgment the collections cannot be taken up conveniently by other trustworthy persons. In order to safeguard the seclusion of conventual life

[57] Cf. Jorder, "Das Sammeln von Almosen durch Ordensfrauen,"—*AKKR*, LXXVI (1896), 105–109.

[58] "Quod vero attinet ad modum in quaeritanda stipe servandum et ad disciplinam a quaestuantibus custodiendam, religiosi utriusque sexus stare debent instructionibus a Sede Apostolica hac de re datis."—Canon 624.

the sisters should avoid, if possible, collecting in person. If the bishop deems their collecting of alms necessary, he is to restrict their collecting to the diocese, if possible, and only for justifiable causes may he permit them to seek alms in another diocese.

3. Every permission for the collecting of alms must be given gratuitously and in writing. The letters are to stipulate the rules and conditions which are to be observed. Permission may be withdrawn at any time, and if the sisters cause any disturbance they are forthwith to be sent back to their convent.

4. Superioresses may, without having obtained the permission of the Ordinary, and provided that the needs of the community or the pious works entrusted to their charge demand help, accept offerings freely given, and even by means of letters beseech honorable and benevolent persons to make donations.

5. The sisters sent out for the purpose of collecting alms are to be of mature age and judgment. If they collect within the diocese they are not to remain outside the convent for more than a month, and if they collect outside the diocese for not more than two months. They are not to be sent out again until either one or two months respectively have elapsed. They are to be provided with sufficient funds to make their return to the convent possible upon the shortest notice.

6. The sisters collecting alms shall not travel alone, nor after dark, nor shall they frequent taverns or other places which may detract from the modesty befitting their religious state. If they are to collect in another diocese, the Ordinary of that place shall be opportunely informed, so that he may provide living accommodations for them either with pious institutes of women or in homes of respectable lay women. The sisters shall conscientiously recite their morning and evening prayers, daily assist at the Sacrifice of the Mass, and receive the Sacraments at least once a week. For the rest, they are to abide by the particular instructions which the superiors may deem necessary to give.

(*b*) *The Decree "De eleemosynis colligendis" of November 21, 1908*[59]

In the introduction of the decree "*De eleemosynis colligendis*"

[59] *AAS*, I (1909), 153–156; *Fontes*, n. 4391.

the Sacred Congregation of Religious stressed the necessity of setting up definite norms governing the collecting of alms by religious institutes of men. The bishops indeed had means of suppressing, either directly or indirectly, any abuses connected with the quest for alms through the many letters and decrees issued by the Holy See in the course of time. Furthermore, the decree "*Singulari quidem*" of March 27, 1896, containing the rules to be observed by women religious, could be employed as directive norms. Yet there was lacking a digest of that cumulative legislation which would be of assistance in checking and suppressing many forms of evil that could arise in connection with the collecting of alms.

The lack of uniform modes of authorization still enabled impostors to collect money from the charitably disposed, and induced some members of religious orders to continue collecting in a manner which caused a consistent departure from the religious spirit, thereby reflecting discredit upon the religious institutes.[60]

Furthermore, problems relative not only to the specified territory in which alms could be collected, but also to the amount of time that could be allotted to such a mission remained to be settled. Heiner (1849–1919), in an article entitled "*Das Kollektieren seitens der Ordensleute,*"[61] enumerated some of the problems with which the bishops were confronted. Among these problems he included the not infrequent case of clerics being commissioned to collect alms for months at a time, even though they were still pursuing their theological studies in preparation for the reception of the priesthood. Some religious collected throughout different dioceses, even throughout an entire country, before returning to the religious community. Bishops had other charitable institutions in their dioceses which needed the generous help of the local faithful. The existence of these charitable undertakings was sometimes endangered by religious coming from outside the diocese and collecting alms at random. Moreover, to be absent from the community, away from the supervision of a superior and the companionship of fellow religious, could not but produce

60 "Members of Religious Orders Collecting Funds,"—*ER,* XL (1908), 412.

61 *AKKR,* XCI (1911), 95–110; cf. in particular pp. 99–101.

detrimental effects on the spirituality of the collectors themselves.

It was for the benefit of the religious institutes as well as that of the bishops in governing their dioceses that the Sacred Congregation of Religious prescribed definite rules which would in the future control the collecting of alms by institutes of men religious, as it had already done regarding the collecting of alms by institutes of women religious.

The norms of this decree recapitulated previous legislation, and formed the basis for the present legislation in the Code of Canon Law on alms-gathering by religious.[62] The decree is divided into two sections: (1) norms for the mendicant orders, and (2) norms for the non-mendicant orders and other religious institutes. They are summarized as follows:

1. Regulars who are called mendicants and are such by Apostolic constitution have the privilege of collecting without the permission of the Ordinary in any diocese in which they have a convent. They require only the authorization of their own religious superior, since the fact that the institute was established in the diocese by the permission of the Ordinary is acknowledged as sufficient approval on the part of the diocesan authorities of the methods whereby the community receives its support. This privilege, however, is enjoyed only when the collecting of alms is undertaken by the regulars themselves.

2. If the above-mentioned regulars wish to collect in a diocese in which no convent of theirs is situated, they must obtain through their superior the permission of the Ordinary of that diocese in writing. Once granted, this permission is good until expressly revoked.

3. Religious superiors shall entrust this office only to those who are of mature age and judgment, and never select those who are pursuing their theological studies. Unless a reasonably grave cause intervenes, the collectors shall not solicit alms alone, but in pairs. When it is necessary for them to remain outside their monastery they are to reside with pastors or in houses belonging to religious. The period allotted to them for the collecting of alms is to be specifically stated, and no members of the order can

[62] Canons 621–624.

continue the quest longer than one month at a time in their own diocese, or for longer than two months outside the diocese. Upon their return they must lead the regular community life for a month, or two months respectively, before being sent out on a similar mission.

4. If religious should fail in observing the injunctions prescribed and cause scandal among the faithful, local Ordinaries can order them back to the monastery and demand that the superior punish them according to the gravity of their delinquency. If the superior fails, then the bishop is to report the matter as soon as possible to the Holy See.

5. Religious orders and congregations of pontifical approval which do not possess the privilege of collecting alms in virtue of their approved Constitutions, or in virtue of an apostolic concession for the possession of which proof must be furnished by reliable documents, cannot collect alms without first having obtained the explicit permission of the Holy See. In addition, they must seek the permission of the local Ordinary, unless it is specifically stated otherwise in the apostolic grant. If they wish to collect in another diocese they need in addition the permission of that Ordinary obtained in writing.

6. Religious of diocesan approval need the explicit permission of their own bishop and also that of the Ordinary of any other diocese wherein they may want to collect alms. Permission for all non-mendicants shall not be lightly granted, particularly if mendicant houses already exist in the diocese.

7. Religious who wish to collect for the foreign missions must possess letters of authorization from the apostolic vicars or prefects of the respective missionary fields, similar letters from their own religious superiors, and a recent and authentic document issued by the Sacred Congregation of the Propagation of the Faith.

8. The norms prescribed regarding the discipline to be observed are the same as those for the mendicants. The office of alms-gathering shall be assigned to those religious who are of mature age and judgment, and they are to collect in pairs, unless a grave cause intervenes. When collecting outside the locality of their monastery they are to reside with pastors or in houses which belong to religious. They are not to be absent for more than a

month when collecting in their own diocese, or for more than two months when collecting in any other diocese. If they perpetrate any delinquency, local Ordinaries are to order them back to their community, where they are to be punished by their superiors according to the gravity of the offense; and if the latter default, the bishops are to report to the Holy See.

Article 4

ORIENTAL ALMS-COLLECTORS

Not infrequently have the Supreme Pontiffs made efforts to check abuses of Orientals in the collecting of alms. Among the early documents on Oriental alms-collectors there is the decree of Innocent XI (1676–1689) "*Cum sancta,*" of February 4, 1677,[63] in which decree all Greek Orientals, seculars as well as ecclesiastics including regulars, were forbidden to collect alms under any pretext whatsoever. Only in rare cases and for exceptional reasons did this decree permit the Sacred Congregation of the Propagation of the Faith to derogate from its provisions.

Subsequently, the Constitutions of Alexander VIII (1689–1691)[64] and Clement XII (1730–1740)[65] restated and reaffirmed the decree of Innocent XI. Both popes strongly protested the abuses prevalent everywhere, and decreed that Orientals, whether of the secular or religious clergy, should not seek alms without the explicit permission of the Sacred Congregation of the Propagation of the Faith.

On the 24th of September, 1882, this same Congregation issued an encyclical letter,[66] which in particular affected Oriental alms-collectors in America. This decree again definitely prescribed the special permission of the Holy See for all Orientals who wished to collect alms. If any collectors appeared without this special authorization they were to be forbidden the exercise of the sacred

---

[63] *Bullarium Pontificium S. Congregationis de Propaganda Fide* (5 vols., Romae, 1839–1841), I, 230.

[64] "*Alias emanavit,*" 21 oct. 1690—*BRT*, XX, 145.

[65] "*Dudum emanavit,*" 26 mart. 1736—*BRT*, XXIV, 163.

[66] "*Soviente avviene,*"—*Collectanea S. Congregationis de Propaganda Fide* (2 vols., Romae, 1907), n. 1575. Hereafter cited as *Collectanea.*

ministry. The regulations were clear. Local Ordinaries were entitled to see the rescript to verify its authenticity and the identity of the persons collecting.

In an encyclical letter a few years later [67] this Sacred Congregation recalled some unedifying facts. It had happened that some Oriental clerics who were sent for the spiritual care of the faithful in America, and other territories of the Latin rite where Orientals had settled, neglected their mission; others indeed collected alms, but without authorization from or regard for local authorities. The conduct of such Orientals became a source of public scandal to the faithful, and rather lowered esteem for the clergy. American bishops complained about the abuses. At times they were at a loss what to do. Some Orientals presented documents which were written in a strange foreign language and thus remained undecipherable. Ordinaries repeatedly were unable to discern whether the persons in question were Catholic or schismatic priests, whether or not they were free from censures, or whether perhaps laymen represented themselves as priests by showing false documents when they sought permission for begging.

The Sacred Congregation of the Propagation of the Faith, in addition to providing the procedure to be followed by all Oriental priests who wished to serve the missions in America, further stipulated that the prohibition of collecting alms without proper authorization should remain intact. Priests who acted contrary to these provisions were not to be admitted to exercise their sacred ministry.[68]

Complaints of lay people and ecclesiastics about the large and unwarranted number of priests, secular and religious, who came from abroad to collect alms drew the attention of the Fathers of the III Plenary Council of Baltimore (1884).[69] The Fathers of the Council stated that not a few of the immigrants collected

---

[67] "*Relatum est,*" 12 apr. 1894—*Collectanea,* n. 1866.

[68] Cf. Duskie, *The Canonical Status of the Orientals in the United States* (The Catholic University of America Canon Law Studies, no. 48, Washington, D. C.: The Catholic University of America, 1928), pp. 36–37.

[69] *Acta et Decreta Concilii Plenarii Baltimorensis Tertii* (Baltimorae, 1886), n. 295.

without permission of the Ordinaries, and even dared to scorn the prohibition of Ordinaries and priests, thus causing general scandal and detriment to their own pious causes. The Council of Baltimore accordingly decreed that priests who came from abroad without proper authorization to collect alms were not to be permitted to say Mass, not even once, without the permission of the local Ordinary.[70]

Despite the efforts made by the Supreme Pontiffs and others to eradicate abuses of Oriental alms-collectors, whether laymen or ecclesiastics, secular or religious, abuses continued. These collectors, according to the Circular Letter of the Sacred Congregation of the Propagation of the Faith on January 1, 1912,[71] usually came fortified with documents which they claimed were written and sealed by prelates and even by patriarchs. The letters recommended the collectors for their probity and integrity of life, and testified that they were commissioned to solicit alms for the construction and repair of churches; for the erection and support of schools, hospitals and orphanages; sometimes for the relief of the needy; and in general for pious enterprises. Frequently it happened that the documents were apocryphal, that the men themselves were not ecclesiastical persons, but only feigned to be such by wearing priestly and religious garb. Often alms were collected for the personal gain of the collectors, and not for the charitable causes which were so solemnly proclaimed. Briefly the instruction of the Sacred Congregation in this matter is as follows:

1. Ordinaries shall not admit into their diocese any member of an Oriental rite for the purpose of collecting alms, regardless of what order or ecclesiastical dignity he pretends to enjoy, and no matter what documents he presents, unless he possesses an authentic and recent rescript of the Sacred Congregation which authorizes him to leave his country for the purpose of collecting alms.

2. If it should happen that a collector of an Oriental rite, even though fortified with a letter of recommendation from his prelate,

---

[70] This decree, however, excepted regulars when saying Mass privately in monasteries of their own order.—*Op. cit.*, n. 295.

[71] *AAS*, IV (1912), 532–533.

should visit Europe, America, or any other region contrary to the provisions made by the Sacred Congregation, the bishop of the place where he happens to be shall warn him that his collecting is forbidden, and shall prevent him from saying Mass or exercising any ecclesiastical function.

3. Should the collector of the Oriental rite fail to heed the admonition, then the Ordinary shall notify the clergy and the faithful that his soliciting of alms is carried on unlawfully.

4. In case of doubt the Ordinary shall consult the Sacred Congregation before giving his approval.

PART II

CANONICAL COMMENTARY

INTRODUCTORY REMARKS

In the historical conspectus of this work it was noted that alms-gathering by religious is juridically and technically a privilege granted to religious institutes whereby their members either personally or through others go from place to place seeking alms for their sustenance and for the promotion of pious and charitable works entrusted to their care. The collecting of alms, though practised by individuals and by groups of the faithful from the very beginning, first became common in the twelfth and thirteenth centuries with the rise of the mendicant orders, and with the general movement towards a stricter observance of evangelical poverty as counselled by Christ. Since that period there have been frequent legislative enactments of the Church governing alms-gathering by religious. Definite norms were formulated for religious institutes of women in the decree "*Singulari quidem*" of March 27, 1896, and for religious institutes of men in the decree "*De eleemosynis colligendis*" of November 21, 1908. These two decrees formed the basis for the present legislation on alms-gathering by religious in the Code of Canon Law.

In the commentary consideration will be given to the present legislation on alms-gathering by religious under the following captions: (1) the right and privilege of alms-gathering by mendicants in the strict sense; (2) alms-gathering by religious who are not mendicants in the sense of canon 621; (3) personal qualifications—methods and discipline to be observed in alms-gathering; (4) alms-gathering by Orientals.

CHAPTER IV

THE RIGHT AND PRIVILEGE OF ALMS-GATHERING BY MENDICANTS IN THE STRICT SENSE

There remain from the middle ages four great mendicant orders which were already recognized as such by the II Council of Lyons in 1274.[1] They are the Order of Preachers, the Friars Minor, the Carmelites, and the Hermits of St. Augustine. Successively other orders and congregations obtained in whole or in part the privileges of the mendicant orders, but the Council of Trent (1545–1563) granted the right of proprietorship to all orders and congregations, with only two exceptions, which had not already obtained the right to ownership through apostolic concession. Only the Friars Minor of the strict observance and the Capuchins were exempted from this general concession.[2] The latter thereby retain their original status of strict mendicancy.[3]

With certain restrictions the Jesuits and the Discalced Carmelites fall under the classification of strict mendicancy.[4] Thus the Jesuits in virtue of their professed houses, and also of residences which are compared to professed houses, are truly mendicants in the strict sense;[5] thus also among the Discalced Carmelites houses not destined for the missions may have income only in exceptional cases.[6] Such actual mendicancy, however, does not

---

[1] Mansi, XXIV, 96.

[2] Sess. XXV, *de regularibus*, c. 3; cf. Schaefer, *De Religiosis*, n. 51 sub 5.

[3] Pius V, const. "*Etsi mendicantium*," 16 maii 1567—*Fontes*, n. 121.

[4] Mannucci, "De Iure et Ratione Quaestuandi,"—*Analecta Ecclesiastica*, XVII (1909), p. 75. Hereafter this article of Mannucci will be cited without reference to the source. Cf. also O'Brien, *Exemption of Religious in Church Law*, p. 246; Wernz-Vidal, *Ius Canonicum*, III, n. 25; Schaefer, *De Religiosis*, n. 429; Beste, *Introductio in Codicem*, p. 422.

[5] Pius V, const. "*Dum indefessae*,"—7 iul. 1571—*BRT*, VII, 923; Creusen-Garesché-Ellis, *Religious Men and Women in the Code* (3. ed., Milwaukee: Bruce, 1940), n. 320. Hereafter cited as Creusen, *Religious Men and Women in the Code*.

[6] *Regulae et Constitutiones Fratrum Discalceatorum Ordinis Beatissimae*

necessitate entire reliance for the actual daily sustenance on alms collected from door to door.[7]

Article 1

MENDICANTS IN THE SENSE OF CANON 621

> **Canon 621, § 1: Regulares, qui ex instituto mendicantes vocantur et sunt, eleemosynas in dioecesi, ubi eorum religiosa domus est constituta, quaerere valent de sola Superiorum licentia . . .**

Canon 621 deals exclusively with alms-gathering by members of religious institutes who are mendicants in name and in fact, and gives them the right *ipso iure* to solicit alms within the diocese in which their religious house is established.

Today only such are mendicants in name and in fact who, in virtue of their original Rule or Constitutions approved by the Holy See, profess absolute poverty and disclaim every right to proprietorship not only individually but also in common.[8]

Formerly there could have been reason to question the meaning of the phrase in canon 621, "*qui ex instituto mendicantes vocantur et sunt,*" for it was not absolutely clear whether those mendicants were included who in virtue of their pristine Rule and Constitutions had no claim to ownership of property, but in virtue of the Council of Trent or apostolic indult were granted the right to such ownership in common.[9] The Commission for the authentic interpretation of the Code has definitely settled the matter, and its meaning can no longer be questioned.[10]

Virginis De Monte Carmelo (Romae: Typis Polyglottis Vaticanis, 1928), n. 19; Larraona in *CpR,* XII, (1931), 251, sub nota 464.

[7] Creusen, *loc. cit.;* Vermeersch-Creusen, *Epitome Iuris Canonici,* I, n. 782.

[8] Schaefer, *De Religiosis,* n. 429; Coronata, *Institutiones Iuris Canonici ad Usum Utriusque Cleri et Scholarum* (5 vols., Taurini: Marietti, 1928–1936, Vols. I–II, 2. ed., 1939), I, n. 1101 (Hereafter cited as *Institutiones Iuris Canonici*). Fanfani, *De Iure Religiosorum,* n. 358; O'Brien, *Exemption of Religious in Church Law,* p. 246.

[9] . . . "Members of Religious Orders Collecting Funds"—*ER,* XL (1911), 412–417.

[10] 16 oct. 1919, ad 10—*AAS,* XI (1919), 478.

The Code Commission was asked whether canon 621, § 1, is to be understood as applying only to religious who are mendicants in the strict sense, or whether it applies also to those who are called such in a wider sense, as, for example, the Order of Preachers; and if the reply is to be in the affirmative to the first part: whether the aforementioned mendicants need the permission of the local Ordinary if they wish to collect money in the diocese for the construction, ornamentation, etc., of their churches. The reply was as follows:

In the affirmative to the first part, namely that canon 621, § 1, extends only to those who are mendicants in virtue of their foundation and in fact are such; in the negative to the second part, that is, mendicants in the wider sense follow the provisions of canon 622 which govern institutes of pontifical right. As regards the obtaining of permission from the local Ordinary, that is provided for in the above cited canon 621, § 1.[11]

This response from the Commission for the authentic interpretation of the Code does not invalidate privileges granted to other mendicant orders and congregations. These privileges as contained in approved Constitutions, or as granted by special apostolic Indult, prevail even though such religious institutes claim the right to proprietorship. Such, for example, is the case with the Minor Conventuals,[12] the Discalced Brethren of the Order of the Most Holy Trinity,[13] and others.[14]

---

[11] Cf. Bouscaren, *The Canon Law Digest* (2 vols., Milwaukee: Bruce Publishing Company, 1934–1943), I, 323.

[12] In their Constitutions approved after the promulgation of the Code the following is given on alms-gathering: "Fratres nostri in dioecesi, ubi eorum domus religiosa est constituta, eleemosynas quaerere valent, de sola Superiorum licentia quam secum scripto semper deferant ad molestias praecavendas (cn. 621, § 1); extra dioecesim vero indigent praeterea, nisi adsit legitima consuetudo, licentia scripto data ab Ordinario loci, in quo eleemosynas colligere cupiunt."—*Constitutiones Ordinis Fratrum Minorum Sancti Patris Francisci Conventualium* (Romae: Ad SS. XII Apostolos, 1932), n. 508.

[13] In their Constitutions approved after the promulgation of the Code the following is given on ams-gathering: "Religiosi eleemosynas in dioecesi, ubi domus est constituta, quaerere valent de sola superioris immediati licentia; extra dioecesim vero indigent praeterea licentia scripto data ab Ordinario, in quo eleemosynas colligere cupiunt."—*Regula Primitiva et*

Article 2

THE RIGHT OF ALMS-GATHERING IN THE DIOCESE IN WHICH THE RELIGIOUS HOUSE IS SITUATED

Mendicants who are such in name and in fact may solicit alms with the sole permission of their superior within the diocese in which their house is situated.[15] This is an innate and inherent right which such religious have independently of all other religious irrespective of their status. Juridically this right rests in the very nature of the religious institute in that it professes absolute poverty and depends upon personal labor and the uncertain income from mendicancy for its own subsistence and for the support of pious and charitable works entrusted to its care.[16]

The local Ordinary has no control over the practice of mendicancy by these institutes directly, but only indirectly in so far as he has the right to determine whether or not such a religious house shall be established in his diocese.[17] He is held to have given his permission implicitly and necessarily in the very act whereby he gave his consent to the establishment of such a mendicant house in his diocese.[18] This is likewise apparent from the decree of the Sacred Congregation of Religious "*De eleemosynis colligendis,*" issued on November 21, 1908, from which decree the canons of the Code on alms-gathering by religious were substantially taken. In it is stated the following: *Ordinariorum licentia necessario censenda est data in ipso actu quo conventus fundationi consensum praebuerunt.*[19] It is also in this sense that the Sacred Congregation had answered previous doubts in this matter.[20]

Constitutiones Fratrum Discalceatorum Ordinis Sanctissimi Trinitatis Redemptionis Captivorum (Isola del Liri: Soc. Tip. a Maioce & Pisani, 1933), n. 63.

[14] Cf. Schaefer, *De Religiosis,* n. 429.

[15] Canon 621, § 1.

[16] Cf. Chapter I, Art. II, *supra.*

[17] Canons 496; 497, § 1, § 2.

[18] Beste, *Introductio in Codicem,* p. 421; Schaefer, *De Religiosis,* n. 429.

[19] *AAS,* I (1909), 153, I, 1; *Fontes,* n. 4391.

[20] ". . . cum in erectione Monasteriorum haec licentia eis tacite ab Ordinariis impertita censeatur."—Ferraris, *Prompta Bibliotheca,* s.v. "*Eleemosyna,*" n. 35; Heiner, "Das Kollektieren seitens der Ordensleute,"—*AKKR,* XCI (1911), 104.

However, the words *religiosa domus* of canon 621 must be taken in their most obvious sense, as meaning only a canonically erected house. Certainly when a bishop grants permission to mendicant religious to establish a parish, or also a school or a hospital in his diocese, his permission for the soliciting of alms cannot be presumed as it can when he gives permission for the erection of a house in the canonical sense of canon 497, § 1. His consent is, therefore, given only when he consents to the establishment of a canonically established house as the provision of the decree *"De eleemosynis colligendis"* indicates: *Ordinariorum licentia necessario censenda est data in ipso actu quo conventus fundationi consensum praebuerunt.*[21]

The right of individual religious to the exercise of this privilege depends upon the religious superior himself. Canon 621, § 1, explicitly demands the permission of the religious superior. It is left to his judgment to determine its necessity, the time and the localities in which the religious may collect alms.[22]

The question may be raised as to what superior is entitled to grant the permission for collecting alms. The Code uses the expression *licentia Superiorum suorum.* If the Constitutions of the religious institute do not specify otherwise, then these words imply reference also to the local superior.[23]

By local superior, however, is meant only the superior of a *domus* in the formal technical sense of canon 497, § 1. That is to say, the expression *licentia Superiorum suorum* applies only to the local superiors of a house for which the approval of the Apostolic See and the written consent of the local Ordinary are necessary for valid erection, whether that house be formal or not. It could not and does not apply to the superior of a *domus* in the wide material sense of a house in which religious mendicants happen to be residing, such as the superior of a hospital or the superior of a school, or a mere parish residence.

---

[21] I, 1; cf. Mannucci, "Commentarium Statuorum de Quaestuatione,"—*Analecta Ecclesiastica,* XVII (1909), 8.

[22] Mannucci, "De Iure et Ratione Quaestuandi," p. 79.

[23] Clancy, *The Local Religious Superior* (The Catholic University of America Canon Law Studies, no. 175, Washington, D. C.: The Catholic University of America Press, 1943), p. 68; Blat, *Commentarium Textus Codicis Iuris Canonici* (5 vols. in 6, Romae, 1920–1927), II, 689.

Neither the Code nor the decree of the Holy See indicates that the power to grant permission to solicit alms is restricted to superiors higher than the superior of a canonically established house. Only when this power has been specifically reserved to higher superiors by the Constitutions is the phrase *licentia Superiorum suorum* to be understood in this sense. There is no reason to question the assertion that the Constitutions of a particular institute may require that the permission of a provincial or higher superior be obained by local superiors in the event that they wish to send their subjects into another diocese to solicit alms.

The power of the superior who enjoys the right to grant permission to solicit alms without the consent of the local Ordinary extends only to the diocese in which the canonically erected house is situated, and to which the religious themselves belong either through profession or residence.[24]

For greater clarity the following conclusions arising from this restriction may be noted:

1. The religious superior may not send his subjects out to solicit alms in another diocese without the consent of the local Ordinary of the latter, even though the religious may be stationed there in houses which do not require canonical erection.

2. He may not send them into another diocese without the consent of the local Ordinary of the latter, even though another house of their order is canonically erected there, as long as the religious themselves do not belong to that house by profession or residence.

3. He may not send them into another diocese without the consent of the local Ordinary of the latter, even though another religious house of their order was once canonically established there, but is now suppressed.

4. The provincial superior, although not residing in the diocese, may grant such religious the permission to collect alms in the diocese in which is located the canonically erected house to which they are attached. The provincial superior, however, may not send them into another diocese without the consent of the local Ordi-

---

[24] O'Brien, *Exemption of Religious in Church Law,* p. 246.

nary of the latter, even though the latter diocese is within the territory of the religious province.

The permission of the religious superior need not necessarily be in writing when the collection is taken up in the diocese in which the canonically erected house is situated, though it must be in writing when he sends such religious into another diocese.[25] In practice, however, religious who solicit alms even in their own legitimate territory should carry with them the written commission of their superior. Through such a document the local Ordinary, pastors and others can readily distinguish them from such as have no right to solicit alms in the diocese. Frequently the Constitutions demand this letter.[26]

In order that mendicant religious may enjoy the privilege of canon 621 they must undertake the task personally, and not through others. The decree "*De eleemosynis colligendis*" states: *Ut mendicantes praefato iure gaudeant, per seipsos, non autem per personas Ordini extraneas, eleemosynas colligere debent.*[27]

It seems that this provision of the decree is effective today. It is a *modus agendi* and disciplinary in character, and is at least implicitly contained in the Code in virtue of canon 624. Canon 624 states that in the method and discipline to be observed in almsgathering, religious of both sexes must obey the instructions which the Holy See has issued in the matter.[28]

The reason for such legislation can readily be understood in view of the countless abuses which would otherwise arise; then also the privilege is of its very nature something personal and is based upon the very poverty which the religious institute professes. The religious founders themselves recommended this practice to the brethren as a suitable means of advancing in the

---

[25] Cf. Decretum, "*De eleemosynis colligendis,*" I, 1 and I, 6; *Fontes,* n. 4391; cf. Schaefer, *De Religiosis,* n. 429.

[26] "Fratres nostri in dioecesi, ubi eorum domus religiosa est constituta, eleemosynas quaerere valent, de sola Superiorum licentia quam secum scripto semper deferant ad molestias praecavendas . . ."—*Constitutiones Ordinis Fratrum Minorum Sancti Patris Francisci Conventualium,* n. 508.

[27] I, 5; cf. Schaefer, *De Religiosis,* n. 429.

[28] "Quod vero attinet ad modum in quaeritanda stipe servandum et ad disciplinam a quaestuantibus custodiendam, religiosi utriusque sexus stare debent instructionibus a Sede Apostolica hac de re datis."—Canon 624.

virtues, particularly in the virtues of humility, patience, and self-abnegation.[29] It was for this reason that the collecting of alms by members of religious institutes was sanctioned by the Church.[30]

From the answer of the Commission for the authentic interpretation of the Code [31] it is now clear that the religious in fulfilling their mission can solicit for the needs of their own community and for the support of pious and charitable works entrusted to the care of the religious community. Thus they may solicit for the needs of their churches, schools and other charitable establishments; in general they may solicit whatever is necessary for their erection, ornamentation and preservation, even if such buildings are situated in other dioceses.[32]

The privilege of alms-gathering includes also the prerogative of soliciting alms for an association which is attached to the religious house or the church adjoining it, even if the association is not constituted as an organic juridic body, as long as it properly pertains to the respective religious organization.[33] However, collections taken up for all other associations and confraternities require the consent of the local Ordinary, to whom an exact account of the offerings and expenditures of the funds solicited must be given.[34]

If religious wish to solicit alms for any pious or ecclesiastical purpose not their own they do not enjoy the privilege of alms-gathering as outlined in canons 621–624, but must unquestionably follow the provisions of canon 1503, which forbids private individuals, both clerics and laymen, to collect alms for any charitable or ecclesiastical purpose without the written permission of the

---

[29] Heiner, "Das Kollektieren seitens der Ordensleute"—*AKKR,* XCI (1911), 105.

[30] Heiner, *loc. cit.*

[31] 16 oct. 1919—*AAS,* XI (1919), 479.

[32] Schaefer, *De Religiosis,* n. 429.

[33] Canon 686, § 3, together with canon 497, § 2; Schaefer, *loc. cit.* Cf. Borkowski, *De Confraternitatibus Ecclesiasticis* (The Catholic University of America Canon Law Studies, no. 3, Washington, D. C.: The Catholic University of America, 1918), pp. 94–105.

[34] Canon 691; Schaefer, *loc. cit.*

Holy See or of their own proper Ordinary and of the Ordinary of the place where the collection is to be made.[85]

Today alms-gathering, understood in the juridical technical meaning of canons 621–624,[86] is not as extensively practised as in previous centuries, not even by mendicants who are such in name and in fact. What is to be said of the many other means employed whereby funds are solicited, such as collections taken up in churches and at large assemblies, charity boxes placed at the entrance of churches, petitions through letters, periodicals, and similar methods?

It seems that apart from petitions through letters and periodicals, or assistance from one or even several benefactors,[87] religious, even mendicant in the strict sense when they solicit aid in their own legitimate territory, are governed by the provisions of canon 1503 whenever they collect alms in a manner which is to be considered distinct from the kind of alms-gathering which is defined according to the juridic concept outlined in canons 621–624. Therefore, if religious wish to solicit funds by taking up collections in churches of the diocese, at public gathering places, or through similar methods, they must possess a rescript from the Holy See, or the written permission of their own proper Ordinary and the written consent of the Ordinary of the place where such collections are sought. By strict interpretation religious do not

---

85 "Salvis praescriptis can. 621–624, vetantur privati tam clerici quam laici sine Sedis Apostolicae aut proprii Ordinarii et Ordinarii loci licentia, in scriptis data, stipem cogere pro quolibet pio aut ecclesiastico instituto vel fine."—Canon 1503. Cf. Schaefer, *loc. cit.;* Beste, *Introductio in Codicem*, p. 421.

86 See Chapter I, Article I, *supra.*

87 Doheny, *Church Property: Modes of Acquisition* (The Catholic University of America Canon Law Studies, no. 41, Washington: The Catholic University of America, 1927), p. 51; Ayrinhac, *Administrative Legislation in the New Code of Canon Law* (London, New York, Toronto: Longmans, Green & Co., 1930), p. 394; Vermeersch-Creusen, *Epitome Iuris Canonici*, II, n. 823; Augustine, *The Pastor according to the New Code of Canon Law* (St. Louis: Herder Book Co., 1924), p. 211. Augustine demands the observance of canon 1503 for all forms of soliciting alms, whether written or oral.

need authorization from parish priests, but courtesy seems to demand a mutual understanding in this matter with them.[38]

Religious who are pastors or vicars may, notwithstanding their vow of poverty, accept, collect, and administer alms offered in any manner for the benefit of their parishioners, or for Catholic schools, or for pious institutions connected with the parish. But this activity is subject to the vigilance of the religious superior if the church belongs to the community; otherwise to the vigilance of the local Ordinary.[39] Religious pastors and vicars, while exercising their rights within the territorial limits of their parishes, act in an official capacity, and not as private individuals. When collecting for non-parochial purposes such religious pastors and vicars are subject to canon 1503.[40]

Article 3

THE RIGHT OF ALMS-GATHERING OUTSIDE THE DIOCESE IN WHICH THE RELIGIOUS HOUSE IS SITUATED

Canon 621, § 1: . . . extra dioecesim vero indigent praeterea licentia scripto data ab Ordinario loci in quo eleemosynas colligere cupiunt.
§ 2: Hanc licentiam Ordinarii locorum, praecipue dioecesium finitimarum, nisi gravibus et urgentibus de causis, ne denegent nec revocent, si religiosa domus ex mendicatione in sola dioecesi, in qua est constituta, vivere nullo modo possit.

If the necessity of subsistence and the furtherance of pious causes demand the soliciting of alms even outside the diocese in which the mendicant house is situated, then the mendicants' privilege cannot be made use of without the consent of the local Ordinary of that diocese in which the collections are sought.[41]

38 Ayrinhac, *op. cit.*, p. 393; Doheny, *op. cit.*, p. 51.

39 Canon 630, § 4.

40 Ayrinhac, *loc. cit.;* Doheny, *loc. cit.*

41 In virtue of a special decree, dated October 1, 1909, the Sacred Congregation of Religious expressly confirmed and approved a former privilege of the Friars Minor which permitted them to solicit alms themselves or through other trustworthy persons everywhere for the upkeep of the Holy Land. The Sacred Congregation explicitly exempted this worthy cause

By local Ordinaries are meant not merely the bishops of dioceses, but also abbots and prelates *nullius*, and their vicars general, administrators and vicars apostolic, according to the norms of canon 198. Thus, in the absence of the bishop, the vicar general can issue the permission to solicit alms to mendicants without a special mandate.[42]

For soliciting outside the diocese in which the religious house is situated the local Ordinary and not the religious superior becomes the judge in determining the right of exercising such a privilege.[43] The local Ordinary is entitled to make diligent inquiry through the petitioner and even through others concerning the necessity of soliciting alms in his diocese. Before granting permission he may make suggestions how this necessity may be relieved in some other manner, particularly if there exist in his diocese other mendicant houses which enjoy such a privilege independently of his consent. Then, too, there may be other pious and charitable causes which perhaps to a great extent depend upon the alms of the faithful for support.[44]

If the local Ordinary realizes that the needs of the community are pressing, and that no grave harm will result to other religious institutes and to pious causes already existing in his diocese, he should not be reluctant to grant the permission, even though the religious come from a distance and not from the adjoining diocese spoken of in canon 621, § 2. By reason of their status of mendicancy the Church is wont to be liberal in this matter.

However, since the exercise of alms-gathering by mendicant religious in a diocese in which their house is not established depends upon the permission of the local Ordinary, they must abide by his instructions. The local Ordinary may restrict them as to territory and time.[45] Thus he may forbid them to enter the lo-

from the Decree, "*De eleemosynis colligendis*" of November 21, 1908.—*AAS*, II (1910), 729-730. This privilege in virtue of canons 4 and 613 obtains today, since canon 621 contains no revocatory clause in abolition of the privileges previously granted.

[42] Canon 368.

[43] Mannucci, "De Iure et Ratione Quaestuandi," p. 78.

[44] Mannucci, *loc. cit.*

[45] Mannucci, *op. cit.*, p. 76.

cality of a mendicant community, and accordingly may permit their collecting only in other parts of the diocese, or he may also impose restrictions as to time and the number of solicitors permitted to undertake this office.[46]

The permission of the local Ordinary should be sought through the religious superior,[47] and granted in writing.[48] The observance of this provision will obviate many difficulties and inconveniences, especially when religious may have come from some distance and even from foreign countries.

When religious are sent by their religious superior into that diocese they should carry with them the written commission of their superior and also an authentic copy of the local Ordinary's permission. When called upon they are to present such documents to Ordinaries, but to pastors they are to show them spontaneously and freely even apart from any positive request.[49]

Adjoining Dioceses

> **Canon 621, § 2: Hanc licentiam Ordinarii locorum, praecipue dioecesium finitimarum, nisi gravibus et urgentibus de causis, ne denegent neve revocent, si religiosa domus ex mendicatione in sola dioecesi, in qua est constituta, vivere nullo modo possit.**

This provision of the canon is intended primarily for the local Ordinaries of dioceses which adjoin the particular diocese in which a mendicant community has its house or monastery. It can easily happen that the members of such a religious house cannot collect sufficient alms for their own subsistence and the support

[46] Mannucci, *loc. cit.*

[47] "Si vero iidem Regulares extra dioecesim, ubi conventus habent, stipem quaeritare velint, Ordinarii illius dioeceseos licentia, per suos Superiores in scriptis obtenta indigent."—Decretum *"De eleemosynis colligendis,"* I, 2.

[48] ". . . extra dioecesim vero indigent praeterea licentia scripto data ab Ordinario loci in quo eleemosynas colligere cupiunt."—Canon 621, § 1.

[49] "Regulares quaestuantes semper secum habere debent litteras authenticas, quibus constet de debita facultate deque officio quaestuationis sibi commisso. Quas litteras parochis ultro exhibere tenentur; necnon Ordinariis, quoties ab ipsis requirantur."—Decretum, *"De eleemosynis colligendis,"* I, 6.

of the pious works entrusted to its care if the diocese is territorially small, or also if it is numerically restricted in the number of the faithful who are able to contribute substantially to their cause.[50]

When such is the case, local Ordinaries shall not lightly deny mendicants of another diocese the privilege of soliciting alms in their dioceses. They must have grave and urgent reasons for refusing the permission. Grave and urgent reasons would be present if other mendicant institutes which are already established in the diocese, or if special diocesan projects, both depending principally upon the generosity of the local faithful, would be jeopardized through the additional exercise of mendicancy.

However, as canon 621, § 2, states, once the permissions have been granted, their revocation in the future is not a matter which may be presumed. To be revoked these permissions must be explicitly withdrawn by the proper authorities, unless a temporal limit is set in the documents wherein these permissions were granted. The reasons for revocation, as the canon states, must also be grave and urgent.

[50] Schaefer, *De Religiosis,* n. 429.

CHAPTER V

ALMS-GATHERING BY RELIGIOUS WHO ARE NOT MENDICANTS IN THE SENSE OF CANON 621

Article 1

religious comprehended under canon 622

Canon 622, § 1: Alii omnes religiosi Congregationum iuris pontificii, sine peculiari Sanctae Sedis privilegio, stipem petere prohibentur; quibus, si hoc privilegium impetraverint, opus erit praeterea licentia scripto data ab Ordinario loci, nisi aliter in ipso privilegio cautum fuerit.

(*a*) *Regulars and Religious of Pontifical Approval*

Canon 622 definitely determines that all other religious of congregations of pontifical approval are forbidden to seek alms without a special privilege of the Holy See. Those institutes which have obtained an Indult need in addition the written permission of the local Ordinary, unless it be expressly stated otherwise in the grant of the privilege.

"**Alii omnes religiosi Congregationum iuris pontificii.**" This expression of canon 622, § 1, is not as generic and comprehensive as the terminology employed in the statutes of the decree "*De eleemosynis colligendis*" of November 21, 1908. That decree stated: *Religiosi sive Ordinum sive Congregationum iuris pontificii, qui privilegium quaeritandi eleemosynas neque vi propriarum Constitutionum a Sancta Sede approbatarum, neque vi Apostolicae concessionis gaudent, veniam Apostolicae Sedis impetrare debent, ut quaestuationes instituere valeant; praeterea licentiam per suos Superiores ab Ordinario loci obtinere tenentur, nisi forte Sancta Sedes in hoc expresse et specialiter iuri Episcopi derogaverit, quod numquam praesumi potest, sed indubitatis documentis probari debet.*[1]

Canon 622, § 1, omits the phrase "*religiosi sive Ordinum.*" In

[1] II, 1—*AAS*, I (1909), 155; *Fontes*, n. 4391.

what category are such regulars to be classified who are not mendicants in name and in fact? From a reply of the Commission for the authentic interpretation of the Code [2] it is now certain that they do not enjoy the privileges of canon 621, unless it can be proved by clear and authentic documents that such have been granted by the Holy See. Nor are such regulars technically and juridically comprehended under the terminology *religiosi Congregationum iuris pontificii.*[3]

There seems to be a *lacuna* in the present legislation. In such an instance canon 20 will form the basis for its analysis and interpretation. If there is no explicit provision concerning some affair in the universal or the particular law, a norm of action is to be taken from the import of laws enacted in similar cases, and from the common and constant teaching of approved authors in the matter.[4]

The decree *"De eleemosynis colligendis"* expressly included regulars who are not mendicants falling within the scope of canon 621, and embodied them under the concept of the class of religious as now specified in canon 622. Authors who touch upon this particular point are commonly agreed that such regulars, unless expressly exempted by their Constitutions or through particular Indult, are to follow the law given for religious of congregations of pontifical approval.[5]

Then too, canon 6, n. 4, strengthens this opinion. When there is doubt whether some provision of the canons differs from the earlier law, the pre-Code law must still be followed.[6]

That regulars in general do not enjoy the privilege of mendicants who are such in the strict sense in the matter of alms-gathering is deducible from reason. The justification of the practice of alms-gathering depends upon necessity. This necessity may arise (a) *per modum status,* as is the case with such re-

[2] 16 oct. 1919—*AAS,* XI (1919), 478.

[3] Cf. canon 487, n. 7.

[4] Cf. canon 20.

[5] Beste, *Introductio in Codicem,* p. 421; Fanfani, *De Iure Religiosorum,* n. 358 sub B; O'Brien, *Exemption of Religious in Church Law,* p. 248.

[6] "In dubio num aliquod canonum praescriptum cum veteri iure discrepet, a veteri iure non est recedendum."—Canon 6, 4°.

ligious whose institutes do not possess any title or right to subsistence except the uncertain income derived from mendicancy; (b) *per modum actus,* as is the case with religious institutes which, though they are entitled to possess movable and immovable property, yet do not derive from such titles a sufficient income for their own subsistence and for the support of the pious and charitable works entrusted to their care. All religious who are not by the state of actual mendicancy entitled to collect alms must therefore justify their claim on some actual concession of the privilege by competent authority.[7]

Consequently, unless special provisions either in the Constitutions as approved by the Holy See, or in a particular apostolic Indult, indicate otherwise, the following religious are subject to the provisions of canon 622, § 1 and § 3:

1. Mendicants who are called such in the wider sense, namely, those who in virtue of their original foundation by Rule or Constitutions were not permitted to possess even in common anything that provided a definite revenue, yet for whom this pristine rigor of poverty has been mitigated, that is, those for whom the use and retention of movable and immovable property has been made lawful either through the general dispensation of the Council of Trent (1543–1565)[8] or through particular apostolic Indults as granted to such religious institutes.[9]

Among these mendicant institutes may be listed the Order of Preachers, the Hermits of St. Augustine, the Calced Carmelites, the Trinitarians, the Servites, the Hospitallers of St. John of God, the Hermits of St. Francis de Paul, and others.[10]

2. Mendicants who are called such in an improper sense inasmuch as the privileges of mendicants in general have been given to them by way of inter-communication of privileges among religious institutes. Such are the Cistercians, the Camaldulese, the Theatines, the Camillians (Ministers of the Sick), and others.[11]

---

[7] Mannucci, "De Iure et Ratione Quaestuandi," p. 75.

[8] Sess. XXV, *de regularibus,* c. 3.

[9] Schaefer, *De Religiosis,* n. 51 sub 5; Beste, *Introductio in Codicem,* p. 308.

[10] Schaefer, *loc. cit.*

[11] Schaefer, *loc. cit.*

3. Non-mendicants, that is, religious who in virtue of their original foundation and Rule were always permitted to possess property in common, such as the Benedictines.[12]

4. All religious belonging to congregations of pontifical approval. Here are understood all religious institutes of men and women in which simple vows, whether temporary or perpetual, are pronounced,[13] and which have received the approbation of the Holy See or at least the decree of commendation (*decretum laudis*).[14]

A religious institute is *ab initio* of pontifical approval when established by pontifical authority.[15] Ordinarily when a new institute has developed sufficiently it may ask of the Holy See a positive approbation. Practically the steps of approbation in the Roman Curia are the following: Decree of commendation of the institute;[16] decree of approbation of the new congregation;[17] approbation of the Constitutions, first provisional, then final. Frequently the provisional approval of the Constitutions of the congregation accompanies the approval of the institute.[18] As soon as the decree of commendation is obtained, the institute becomes an institute of pontifical approval [19] and from this moment on the provisions of canon 622, § 1, obtain.

All regulars and religious of congregations of pontifical approval are obliged to seek the privilege of alms-gathering from the Holy See before obtaining the local Ordinary's permission (*licentia*) in writing. The words of the canon are so clear and

---

[12] Schaefer, *loc. cit.*

[13] Canon 488, n. 2.

[14] Canon 488, n. 3.

[15] Schaefer, *loc. cit.*

[16] "Decretum laudis est primus actus, quo Sancta Sedes ad novae Congregationis opus manum ita admovet, ut desinat esse simpliciter dioecesana . . ."—*Normae secundum quas Sacra Congregatio in novis religiosis Congregationibus approbandis procedere solet*—C. I, n. 6—*AAS*, XIII (1921), 312.

[17] *Norm. cit.*, C. I, n. 7.

[18] Creusen, *Religious Men and Women in the Code,* n. 27; Vermeersch-Creusen, *Epitome Iuris Canonici,* I, n. 589.

[19] Cf. Coronata, *Compendium Iuris Canonici* (2 vols., Taurini: Marietti, 1937–1938), I, nn. 885–887; Creusen, *loc. cit.*

absolute that no exception can be made, even though a religious institute may devote its entire activity to the service of the faithful and the welfare of the Church. The fact that people of their own accord request that alms be solicited by religious in the exercise of their activity does not change the law. The privilege must originate solely from the Holy See.[20]

The local Ordinary himself is restricted by the canon. He may grant permission only to those religious who have first obtained the privilege from the Holy See. This privilege may be granted in a general way in the Constitutions or through a special Indult to the entire order or congregation, to a province or even to a particular religious house.[21]

The further need of the permission of the local Ordinary is mandatory. Only when the Holy See in granting this privilege in a special manner derogates from the general rule are religious superiors exempted from seeking the permission of the local Ordinary. When such an exception has been made, it may extend only to the gathering of alms in a diocese in which the religious have a house, and then religious institutes enjoying such a privilege are governed by the rules outlined for mendicants in the strict sense.[22] Thus, for example, the Minor Conventuals[23] and the Discalced Brethren of the Order of the Most Holy Trinity[24] enjoy in virtue of their approved Constitutions the privileges in alms-gathering which mendicants in the strict sense have in consequence of the right established for them by the common law.

(*b*) *Religious Institutes of Diocesan Approval*

Canon 622, § 2: Religiosi Congregationum iuris dioecesani stipem quaeritare nequaquam possunt sine licentia scripto data tum ab Ordinario loci in quo sita

[20] Goyeneche in *CpR,* XI (1930), 81; Schaefer, *De Religiosis,* n. 429.

[21] Heiner, "Das Kollektieren seitens der Ordensleute,"—*AKKR,* XCI (1911), 107.

[22] Canon 621.

[23] *Constitutiones Ordinis Fratrum Minorum Sancti Patris Francisci Conventualium,* n. 508.

[24] *Regula Primitiva et Constitutiones Fratrum Discalceatorum Ordinis Sanctissimae Trinitatis Redemptionis Captivorum,* n. 63.

est eorum domus, tum ab Ordinario loci in quo stipem quaerere cupiunt.

By religious congregations of diocesan approval are understood those religious institutes which have been canonically erected, but which have not as yet obtained the decree of commendation of the Holy See.[25] When the Holy See has issued the decree of commendation to a diocesan religious institute and thus entertains its application for an eventually full pontifical approval it ceases to be diocesan.[26] Up to the time that a decree of commendation is issued the provisions of canon 622, § 2, obtain.

Religious belonging to a house of diocesan approval do not need from the Holy See the grant of the special privilege of seeking alms. They may solicit with the sole permission of their local Ordinary as long as they remain in the diocese where they have their domicile. If such religious desire to seek alms in another diocese, they need in addition the permission of that local Ordinary, as will be noted in the subsequent Article.

Article 2

RIGHTS AND DUTIES OF LOCAL ORDINARIES

Canon 622, § 3: Religiosis, de quibus in §§ 1 et 2 huius canonis, Ordinarii locorum licentiam quaeritandae stipis ne concedant, praesertim ubi sunt conventus regularium nomine et re mendicantium, nisi sibi constet de vera domus vel pii operis necessitate, cui alio modo occurri nequeat; quod si necessitati provideri possit stipe quaerenda intra locum seu districtum vel dioecesim in qua iidem commorantur, ampliorem licentiam ne largiantur.

The rights and duties of local Ordinaries in granting permission for alms-gathering as studied in this Article are not related to the privileges of religious who are mendicants in name and in fact, or to such religious as by their Constitutions or through an apostolic Indult enjoy the same privileges as those who are

[25] Canon 488, n. 3.

[26] Cf. p. 81, *supra*.

mendicants in the strict sense. The relation of these two privileged groups to local Ordinaries, when collecting outside their own diocese, has been considered in the previous chapter. The present consideration is restricted to the following classes: regulars who do not enjoy the above-mentioned privileges of mendicants, religious of congregations of pontifical approval, and religious of congregations of diocesan approval.

(*a*) *Regulars and Religious of Congregations Collecting Within the Diocese*

When regulars and religious of pontifical approval have obtained from the Holy See the privilege of alms-gathering, its exercise still depends upon the prudent judgment of the local Ordinary.[27] The local Ordinary can demand the presentation of the rescript of the Sacred Congregation for recognition and verification.[28]

Upon recognition of such a rescript the local Ordinary can and should make diligent inquiry through the proper religious superior and even through others to ascertain the need of alms in providing for the subsistence of the religious house and the pious works entrusted to its care.[29]

Canon 622, § 3, clearly states that the local Ordinary is not to grant his permission to collect alms if the necessity of the religious house can be taken care of in some other manner. Thus he would certainly be within his right in suggesting that aid be solicited through other means, e.g., through the sending of letters by mail, or through an appeal to potential benefactors.[30]

If in the estimation of the local Ordinary even the collecting of alms will not suffice to sustain the needs of a particular house, he would have a canonical reason for suppressing the house of an institute of diocesan approval after having heard the mod-

---

[27] ". . . opus erit praeterea licentia scripto data ab Ordinario loci, nisi aliter in ipso privilegio cautum fuerit."—Canon 622, § 1.

[28] Cf. canon 51.

[29] Mannucci, "De Iure et Ratione Quaestuandi," p. 75.

[30] Mannucci, *loc. cit.*

erator of that congregation, provided that it be not the only house of that congregation.[31] For other religious houses he may recommend suppression to the supreme moderator or to the Holy See itself.[32]

"Ubi sunt conventus regularium nomine et re mendicantium." When in a diocese are established houses of mendicants who are such in name and in fact, or religious houses which enjoy by special apostolic concession the privilege of mendicants, the local Ordinary should be more reticent of and restrictive in the granting of his permission to other religious houses. Mendicants have an inherent right *per modum status* to depend upon alms for subsistence; other religious are entitled to such help only *per modum actus.*

Thus the local Ordinary can bar non-mendicants from entering a locality where mendicant houses are established.[33] He may restrict the permission for alms-gathering to a certain district, but, on the other hand, he may also give a general concession to solicit everywhere in the diocese, especially if in his judgment the necessity be great and the greater good to the diocese would warrant such general concession.

Besides limitation as to territory the local Ordinary may impose restrictions as to time. The permission may be granted for a year, two years, or even as long as the need of the religious house continues. Then, too, the local Ordinary must adhere to the instructions contained in the rescript of the Holy See. If the rescript is limited, e.g., *ad quinquennium,* the local Ordinary would not be free to extend his permission beyond such a temporal limitation. In such an instance the religious house would be required to obtain a renewal of the privilege from the Holy See before the local Ordinary could grant any further permission.[34]

The permission of the local Ordinary, as in the case of mendicants when soliciting outside their own diocese, should be sought

---

[31] Canon 498 together with canon 493; Mannucci, *loc. cit.*

[32] Mannucci, *loc. cit.*

[33] S. C. Ep. et Reg., 20 iun. 1674—Bizzarri, n. 271.

[34] Mannucci, *loc. cit.*

through the religious superior.[35] The permission must be granted in writing [36] and should be given gratis.[37]

Religious designated for such a commission should carry with them the necessary documents.[38] These documents should include letters of obedience, or the commission of the religious superior designating by name the religious selected for this mission, and at least certified copies of the permission of the local Ordinary and of the rescript of the Holy See.

Unless the local Ordinary has expressly restricted the soliciting of alms for specific purposes, such designated religious may solicit not only for the needs of the religious house itself, but also for all its charitable and pious undertakings.[39] If such religious wish to solicit alms for any other pious or ecclesiastical purpose, they must follow the provisions of canon 1503, which forbids private individuals, both clerics and laymen, to collect alms for any charitable or ecclesiastical purpose without the written permission of the Holy See or of their own proper Ordinary and of the Ordinary of the place where the collection is to be made.[40]

Here again the question may be raised, as noted for mendicant religious,[41] about the many other means sometimes employed whereby funds are solicited, and not comprehended under the juridical and technical concept of alms-gathering as understood in canons 621–624.[42] Such means would include collections taken up in churches and large assemblies, charity boxes placed at the en-

---

[35] "Religiosi . . . praeterea licentiam per suos Superiores ab Ordinario loci obtinere tenentur."—Decretum "*De eleemosynis colligendis,*" II, 1.

[36] Canon 622, § 1.

[37] Decretum "*De eleemosynis colligendis,*" II, 6; Decretum "*Singulari quidem,*" VI; Beste, *Introductio in Codicem,* p. 421.

[38] Regulares (Religiosi) quaestuantes semper secum habere debent litteras authenticas, quibus constet de debita facultate deque officio quaestuationis sibi commisso."—Decretum "*De eleemosynis colligendis,*" I, 6 and II, 9. The word *religiosi* is inserted by writer to signify that II, 9, of the decree refers back to I, 6.

[39] P.C.I., 16 oct. 1919—*AAS,* XI (1919), 478; Schaefer, *De Religiosis,* n. 429.

[40] Schaefer, *De Religiosis,* n. 429; Beste, *Introductio in Codicem,* p. 421.

[41] Pp. 73–74, *supra.*

[42] See Chapter I, Article I, *supra.*

trance of churches, petitions through letters, periodicals, and similar methods.

It seems that apart from petitions through letters and periodicals, or assistance from one or several benefactors,[43] religious, when soliciting for the needs of their community and for pious and charitable undertakings entrusted to their care in a manner distinct from the juridical concept of alms-gathering, follow the provisions of canon 1503. Thus, if religious wish to solicit funds by taking up collections in churches of the diocese, they must possess a rescript to this effect from the Holy See or the written permission of their own proper Ordinary and the written consent of the Ordinary of the place where such collections are sought. When they collect in their own diocese, a rescript of the Holy See is not necessary if the written consent of the local Ordinary has been obtained. If they wish to solicit outside their own diocese, regulars and religious of pontifical approval need the written consent of the local Ordinary of that diocese, and religious of diocesan approval need the additional written permission of their own proper local Ordinary.[44] In strict law religious do not need authorization from parish priests, but courtesy demands at least some mutual understanding in a matter which can affect parochial life and discipline in so intimate a way.[45]

(*b*) *Regulars and Religious of Congregations Collecting Outside the Diocese*

Canon 622, § 3: . . . quod si necessitati provideri possit stipe quaerenda intra locum seu districtum vel dioecesim in qua iidem commorantur, ampliorem licentiam ne largiantur.

Canon 622, § 3, is much more restrictive in permitting regulars and religious of congregations to collect alms outside the diocese

[43] Doheny, *Church Property: Modes of Acquisition*, p. 51; Ayrinhac, *Administrative Legislation in the New Code of Canon Law*, p. 394; Vermeersch-Creusen, *Epitome Iuris Canonici*, II, n. 283; Augustine, *The Pastor according to the New Code of Canon Law*, p. 211.

[44] Authors available to the writer do not discuss this particular point.

[45] Ayrinhac, *op. cit.*, p. 393; Doheny, *op. cit.*, p. 51.

in which their houses are situated than it is with mendicants in the strict sense.[46] Only when sufficient alms cannot be sought in the locality, district, or diocese itself may the local Ordinary grant his permission for the seeking of alms beyond the more restricted area.[47] Such occasions could arise when the needs of a religious house are great, and when the diocese in which it is situated is small, at least relatively so in the number of the faithful from whom alms can be sought.

When regulars and religious of congregations desire to solicit alms outside the dioceses in which their houses are established, they are much like mendicant religious. Even mendicants in the strict sense require the permission of the Ordinary of the diocese in which they wish to solicit alms.[48] The difference consists chiefly in the documents required. From their own diocese mendicant religious need only an authenticated document of commission from their religious superior, whereas all other regulars and the religious of congregations of pontifical approval need the apostolic privilege as well, while institutes of diocesan approval need also the written consent of their own local Ordinary.[49]

Without the presentation of the proper documents, the Ordinary of a diocese in which religious wish to solicit is not obliged to nor should he act in their behalf. Even upon receipt of a fully authorized petition the Ordinary is still empowered either to grant or to deny the request. He may grant it if in his judgment there be true necessity for seeking aid in that manner, and if the permitted soliciting of alms will not prove detrimental either to religious institutes, particularly mendicant already established in his diocese, or to diocesan organizations which may depend upon such means for support. If additional alms-gathering will prove detrimental to the welfare of his diocese, all the remaining fac-

[46] Cf. canon 621.

[47] Cf. Decretum "*Singulari quidem,*" n. 5; Decretum "*De eleemosynis colligendis,*" II, 3.

[48] Canon 621, § 1; Decretum "*De eleemosynis colligendis,*" I, 2.

[49] Mannucci favors the view that all religious who are not mendicants need the permission of their own proper bishop.—"De Iure et Ratione Quaestuandi," p. 76.

tors being equal, he is not only entitled to refuse the permission, but in given cases may have an obligation to do so.[50]

The religious superior shall not send his subjects into another diocese until he has first obtained the permission of that local Ordinary. This will forestall many difficulties and embarrassing situations, especially when religious must come from some distance and even from foreign countries. Upon receipt of this additional permission given in writing, designated religious may solicit alms, carefully adhering to special instructions. They are to carry with them all the indicated necessary documents and to present them when they are requested by the local Ordinary to do so. Even apart from any request they shall always spontaneously and fully submit their papers of authorization to the inspection of the pastors so that these may readily distinguish such religious from those who are not entitled to collect alms.[51]

Article 3

RELIGIOUS INSTITUTES OF WOMEN

The canons of the Code which treat of alms-gathering do not specifically mention religious institutes of women. Nevertheless, in this matter they are governed by the same canons as the religious institutes of men. The dispositions concerning religious, even when expressed in the masculine gender, *religiosus, religiosi,* apply equally to women religious, unless it appears otherwise from the context or from the nature of the case.[52]

In the matter of alms-gathering by religious institutes of women it is important to draw a distinction between (1) nuns who are subject to the papal enclosure, as treated in canons 597–600; (2) nuns who are not subject to the papal enclosure along with sisters (*sorores*), both of whom make a profession of simple vows. For a clear, concise concept of the relation of each

---

[50] Cf. Mannucci, *op. cit.,* p. 77.

[51] "Regulares quaestuantes semper secum habere debent litteras authenticas . . . quas litteras parochis ultro exhibere tenentur; necnon Ordinariis, quoties ab ipsis requirantur."—Decretum *"De eleemosynis colligendis,"* I, 6. Cf. also II, 9, of the same decree.

[52] Canon 490.

group to alms-gathering the following explanation of the distinction between them is useful and necessary.

Nuns (*moniales*) are women religious who profess solemn vows or, unless it appears otherwise from the nature of the case or from the context, women religious whose vows are normally solemn, but which by special disposition of the Holy See are simple in certain places.[53] All women religious who in an order profess vows whether solemn or simple, temporary or perpetual, are nuns.[54] Among these are the Benedictines, the Poor Clares, certain canonesses of St. Augustine, the Carmelites, the Dominicans (of the second order), the Ursulines, the Visitandes, etc.[55]

Nuns whose vows, though according to their institute they should be solemn, are nevertheless only simple in certain regions by order of the Holy See, are not bound by the law of papal enclosure.[56] Since the beginning of the nineteenth century the nuns in France (with the exception of Nice and Savoy) and in Belgium do not take solemn but only simple vows. This is also true in the United States with the exception of a few monasteries of the Visitation and of the second order of St. Dominic.[57]

Sisters (*sorores*) are women religious of institutes in which simple vows are professed.[58] Nuns not subject to the papal enclosure and sisters, both of whom profess simple vows, come under the provisions of canons 621–624 governing alms-gathering by religious.

(*a*) *Nuns Subject to the Papal Enclosure*

Nuns with solemn vows and also nuns who are obliged to the observance of the papal enclosure are not mentioned in the canons governing alms-gathering.[59] In virtue of the laws of their

---

53 Canon 487, n. 7.

54 Schaefer, *De Religiosis,* n. 46; Larraona in *CpR,* IV (1923), 12, cum nota 253; Fanfani, *De Iure Religiosorum,* n. 7; Vermeersch-Creusen, *Epitome Iuris Canonici,* I, n. 593.

55 Creusen, *Religious Men and Women in the Code,* n. 15.

56 P.C.I., 1 mart. 1921—*AAS,* XIII (1921), 77.

57 Creusen, *loc. cit.*

58 Canon 487, n. 7.

59 Schaefer, *De Religiosis,* n. 429.

strict enclosure [60] and the severe penalty provided in law for its violation [61] they are necessarily excluded from the privilege of personally collecting alms. Only in the direst necessity, a matter of life and death, could they ever be permitted to leave the enclosure and solicit such alms absolutely necessary for sustenance; and this only if all other means in the estimation of the local Ordinary proved inadequate.[62]

Nevertheless, the privilege of alms-gathering can be exercised according to the norms of law in their behalf by extern sisters, who profess simple vows, follow the same Rule and Constitutions, and constitute one and the same family.[63]

The Sacred Congregation of Religious in a decree of July 16, 1931, drew up special statutes governing the admission and the mode of life of the extern sisters, who, in the absence of secular persons, are to transact the external business affairs of the monastery. These statutes are of obligation in all monasteries of nuns which have extern sisters by reason of a special approbation of the Holy See.[64]

(b) *Nuns and Sisters Not Subject to the Papal Enclosure*

Women religious who belong to a house which is mendicant in name and in fact, or to a house which in virtue of approved Constitutions or through a special apostolic Indult enjoys the privileges of mendicants in the strict sense, follow the provisions of canon 621. For all other women religious, whether they belong to an order or to a congregation, the provisions of canon 622 hold. Consequently, the commentary, as given for the respective insti-

---

[60] Cf. canons 597–600.

[61] Cf. canon 2342.

[62] Cf. pp. 85–86, *supra;* Pius V, const. "*Decori,*" 1 febr. 1570—*Fontes,* n. 133; Gregorius XIII, const. "*Deo sacris,*" 30 dec. 1572—*BRT,* VIII, 30; Mannucci, "De Iure et Ratione Quaestuandi," p. 74.

[63] Beste, *Introductio in Codicem,* p. 421.

[64] Bouscaren, *The Canon Law Digest,* II, 170; Creusen, *Religious Men and Women in the Code,* n. 16. The text of the statutes of this decree were not published in the *AAS,* but can be found in Schaefer, *De Religiosis,* nn. 654–667.

tutes of men, is likewise applicable to religious institutes of women with the exceptions subsequently noted.[65]

Because of likely impracticabilities or at least inexpediencies which can more readily arise when sisters or nuns collect alms, the Holy See is wont to be slow in approving religious institutes of women which are truly mendicant and accordingly must depend principally on alms for subsistence.[66] This attitude of the Holy See can also be gathered from the norms issued by the Sacred Congregation of Religious on March 6, 1921, as those which it follows in approving new congregations. It urges that the greatest caution must be observed in approving congregations which live solely on alms-gathering.[67]

It seems that nuns with simple vows are obliged to observe the special instructions contained in the Decree "*Singulari quidem*" of March 27, 1896,[68] although in that decree the Sacred Congregation of Bishops and Regulars mentioned only sisters (*sorores*) of institutes with simple vows. For this opinion one can advance the following reasons: (1) No special instructions of the Holy See have been issued which deal with alms-gathering by nuns in simple vows; (2) certain canons of the Code which treat of sisters apply also by analogy of law to nuns.[69] It is for the same reason that the special instructions then issued for sisters were to be considered as applicable also to nuns; (3) the existence of nuns with simple vows is a fact of comparatively recent origin.[70]

For the reasons here alleged, nuns with simple vows who belong to a house which is mendicant in name and in fact, or to a house which in virtue of approved Constitutions or through a

---

[65] Cf. canon 613.

[66] Mannucci, "De Iure et Ratione Quaestuandi," p. 74.

[67] "Cautissime procedendum est in approbandis novis Congregationibus, quae non vivunt nisi ex eleemosynis, atque stipe ostiatim collecta. Approbatis inculcanda est fidelis observantia canonum 622, 613 et 624."—*Normae secundum quas S. Congregatio in novis religiosis Congregationibus approbandis procedere solet*—*AAS* (1921), 312–319, C. II, art. 14.

[68] *ASS*, XXVIII (1895–1896), 555–558.

[69] Schaefer, *De Religiosis*, n. 46; Larraona in *CpR*, IV (1923), 12 cum nota 253.

[70] Cf. p. 90, *supra*.

special Indult enjoys the privileges of mendicants in the strict sense, require the permission of the local Ordinary even when collecting alms in the diocese in which the religious house is established.[71]

Ordinarily the exercise of the privilege of alms-gathering must be undertaken by the religious themselves. At least such is the case when there is question of religious institutes of men.[72] However, the Sacred Congregation of Bishops and Regulars made an exception for religious institutes of women in its decree "*Singulari quidem.*"[73] In this decree the Sacred Congregation stated that the local Ordinary is not to grant sisters the permission to collect alms unless (1) he is assured of the real need of the convent or of the pious and charitable works entrusted to its care, and (2) that the alms cannot be conveniently taken up by other trustworthy persons, designated by the local Ordinary.

It seems that this provision of the decree is effective today. It is a *modus agendi* which is fully disciplinary in character; as a consequence it is at least implicitly contained in the Code in virtue of canon 624.[74] Canon 624 states that in the method and discipline to be observed in alms-gathering, religious of both sexes must obey the instructions which the Holy See has issued in this matter.

The difficulties and dangers which more readily confront women religious in undertaking such an office personally may also be given as a reason why the Holy See issued special norms for religious institutes of women separate and somewhat distinct from those issued for religious institutes of men. This will be noted in the subsequent chapter.

The permission to solicit alms, granted to other trustworthy persons or to the sisters themselves, shall be issued in writing and given gratis. It shall contain commissorial letters to pastors and

[71] Iisdem votorum simplicium Sororibus non liceat eleemosynas quaerere sive intra Dioecesim in qua ipsae resident, sive extra sine licentia Ordinarii loci respectivae residentiae."—Decretum "*Singulari quidem,*" n. 2.

[72] "Ut mendicantes praefato iure gaudeant, per seipsos, non autem per personas Ordini extraneas, eleemosynas colligere debent."—Decretum "*De Eleemosynis colligendis,*" I, 5; Schaefer, *De Religiosis,* n. 428.

[73] N. 5.

[74] Cf. canon 6, n. 6.

other prudent persons in the diocese. They in turn, upon the arrival of the sisters, are to advise and assist them, especially in providing protective hospitality.[75]

If the sisters wish to solicit outside their own diocese, then the local Ordinary in granting permission shall issue commendatory letters to Ordinaries of other dioceses, requesting that they watch over and help them as their own subjects. Only upon the presentation of such documents shall Ordinaries of other dioceses consider their petition. If in their judgment the reasons advanced seem justifiable, they may grant the additional permission.[76]

---

[75] Decretum "*Singulari quidem,*" nn. 6–7.

[76] Decretum, *loc. cit.*

CHAPTER VI

PERSONAL QUALIFICATIONS—METHOD AND DISCIPLINE TO BE OBSERVED IN ALMS-GATHERING

Canon 623: Non licet Superioribus stipem colligendam committere, nisi professis aetate animoque maturis, maxime si de mulieribus agatur, numquam autem iis qui in studia adhuc incumbunt.
Canon 624: Quod vero attinet ad modum in quaeritanda stipe servandum et ad disciplinam a quaestuantibus custodiendam, religiosi utriusque sexus stare debent instructionibus a Sede Apostolica hac de re datis.

Canon 623, dealing with the personal qualifications of religious sent out for alms-gathering, was taken verbatim, with the exception of the phrase "*maxime si de mulieribus agatur*," from the decree of the Sacred Congregation of Religious "*De eleemosynis colligendis*" of November 21, 1908.[1]

The instructions of the Holy See in reference to the method to be followed and the discipline to be observed in alms-gathering are principally contained in the cited decree "*De eleemosynis colligendis*" and in the decree "*Singulari quidem*," issued by the Sacred Congregation of Bishops and Regulars on March 27, 1896, for religious institutes of women.[2] In so far as the instructions of the Holy See treat of the method and discipline to be observed in alms-gathering, they are at least implicitly contained in the Code, and consequently are canonically effective.[3]

Since the method to be followed and the discipline to be observed by men religious is somewhat different from that provided

[1] I, n. 7—*AAS*, I (1909), 153–156; *Fontes*, n. 4391.

[2] *ASS*, XXVIII (1895–1896), 555–558; *Fontes*, n. 2029. Cf. Beste, *Introductio in Codicem*, p. 422; Fanfani, *De Iure Religiosorum*, n. 360; Vermeersch-Creusen, *Epitome Iuris Canonici*, I, n. 782; Schaefer, *De Religiosis*, n. 432.

[3] Cf. canon 6, n. 6.

for women religious, this chapter will treat first of men religious and then of women religious, and finally consider the jurisdictional control of the local Ordinary in the matter which pertains to alms-gathering.

Article 1

PERSONAL QUALIFICATIONS—METHOD AND DISCIPLINE FOR MEN RELIGIOUS

The privilege of alms-gathering is granted to religious institutes by law or by Indult to provide for the general needs of the community. It is granted upon the supposition that this privilege be undertaken by the religious themselves.[4]

Canon 623 clearly states that religious superiors shall entrust this office only to those who are professed, who are of a mature age and mind, who are not engaged in studies. Consequently postulants and novices of a religious house are never to be sent on such a mission. The canon does not restrict the office to those who are in solemn or perpetual vows. For good reasons those who are professed with temporary vows, particularly if they are of a mature age and mind, can be selected. This may be necessary at times in small communities when the perpetually professed may not always be available for this type of work.[5] The determination of the qualifications of the religious who are selected depends upon the prudent judgment of the religious superior. Ordinarily, only such as are professed with solemn or perpetual vows should be chosen.[6]

The Code furthermore demands that the professed religious who are chosen for this office be no longer occupied in studies. It makes no difference whether the studies pursued be sacred, profane, or mixed.[7] The distractions necessarily met in alms-gathering tend to lessen the desire for study and thereby retard the intellectual advancement desirable in a student.

The method to be followed and the discipline to be observed on such a mission is the same for all religious institutes of men.

---

[4] Cf. Chapter IV, Art. II, and Chapter V, Art. III, *supra*.

[5] Schaefer, *De Religiosis*, n. 430.

[6] Mannucci, "De Iure et Ratione Quaestuandi," p. 79.

[7] Schaefer, *loc. cit.*

This is evident from the decree "*De eleemosynis colligendis,*" which in this matter refers the religious who are not mendicants to the provisions outlined for mendicants.[8]

Religious who are sent on a mission to solicit alms are not to go alone, but in pairs, especially outside the city or the place where the convent is situated, unless grave necessity demands otherwise. If a religious is sent alone it is important that he be esteemed by the faithful as commendable for his mature judgment and virtuous life.[9] It is left to the prudent judgment of the religious superior to determine when such grave necessity is present which permits him to send a religious on this mission without a companion. This necessity can easily be present in a small community in which there are but a few professed religious who have the proper qualifications, or even in a larger community in which, on account of the many occupations of the institute, few are available for alms-gathering.[10]

Religious who collect alms within easy access of the convent shall never stay outside their proper house overnight.[11] Whenever they collect outside the vicinity of the convent and are not able to return at night, they shall lodge with pastors, or other priests, be they secular or religious. If this be impossible they are to remain with some pious benefactors noted for Christian uprightness and virtue.[12]

Religious who are sent by their superiors on a mission of alms-gathering shall not remain outside their own religious convent for more than a month when soliciting in their own diocese, or beyond two months when soliciting in strange dioceses. Nor shall the superior subsequently send them on a similar mission until they have lived the religious life in the convent according to their Rules and Constitutions for one or two months respectively, namely, in so far as their mission demanded their living outside

---

[8] "Ad haec et ipsi fideliter observent, quae supra pro Religiosis Ordinum mendicantium sancita sunt, parte I, art. 6, 7, 8, 9, 11, 12, 13."—II, 9.

[9] Decretum "*De eleemosynis colligendis,*" I, 8.

[10] Schaefer, *De Religiosis,* n. 434.

[11] *Decr. cit.,* I, 11.

[12] *Decr. cit.,* I, 9.

the cloister for one month or two months.[13] The provision of this latter statute which requires an interruption of the mission does not seem to apply to religious who solicit within the locality of the convent and return to it in the evening.[14]

Without an apostolic Indult religious superiors may not permit their subjects to remain outside their convent for a longer period of time. The time indicated in the decree is the maximum; if the Constitutions prescribe less, they must be adhered to.[15]

Religious in fulfilling their mission shall always conduct themselves in a manner becoming their state, preserving humility, modesty, and cleanliness. They must avoid all familiarity with people of the world, particularly with people of the other sex, regardless of what may be their condition or state in life. They are to avoid all places which can be considered discreditable to religious. On the contrary, they are to nurture true religious piety, and must fulfill to the best of their ability the spiritual exercises which are customarily fulfilled in their religious community.[16]

Superiors, *graviter onerata eorum conscientia,* shall not omit to give to the collectors before setting out on their mission instructions which prudence and circumstances may dictate.[17] In general, superiors shall indicate those practices which safeguard their subjects' religious vocation and stimulate their zeal for the religious life itself. They shall insist on an exact observance of the laws of the Church, as well as of their Rule and Constitutions. In particular instances special precautions may be necessary, especially if one or the other has caused a disturbance in the past.[18]

The farther the place of collection from the convent and the longer the religious are to be absent from their own community, the more zealous should the interest of the superior be in counselling them. This interest can be shown by correspondence conducted with them at regular intervals, with proper replies sent by

---

[13] *Decr. cit.,* I, 10.

[14] Schaefer, *De Religiosis,* n. 434.

[15] Mannucci, "De Iure et Ratione Quaestuandi," p. 79.

[16] *Decr. cit.,* I, 12.

[17] *Decr. cit.,* I, 13.

[18] Mannucci, "De Iure et Ratione Quaestuandi," p. 79.

the religious in turn to their superior. If anything unexpected should arise the solicitors can thus be the more promptly advised as to what must be done.[19]

The religious collectors, fortified with the instructions and blessing of their superior, shall accept and fulfill their mission in the spirit of faith, collecting alms not for themselves but for Christ, and carefully observing the instructions given them. When the allotted time has elapsed they shall return to their religious house and live the religious life in all its fervor and zeal.

Article 2

PERSONAL QUALIFICATIONS—METHOD AND DISCIPLINE FOR WOMEN RELIGIOUS

The instructions outlined for personal qualifications, method, and discipline to be observed by members of religious institutes of men apply also for the greater part to members of religious institutes of women. Yet, for the sake of fuller clarity it is necessary to point out what is particularly intended for sisters and nuns.

In canon 623 superioresses are in a special manner counselled to send on a mission for alms-gathering only those sisters who are professed, and who are of mature age and character. The canon uses the expression "*maxime si de mulieribus agatur.*" The reason for such caution is evident. With the ever-increasing duty of caring for the needs of charity devolving to a great extent upon religious institutes of women, alms-gathering by them became more necessary and widespread. To forestall any danger of spiritual or physical harm to sisters sent on such missions, the Holy See issued special regulations regarding the selection and regarding the conduct of such sisters.[20]

Neither canon 623 nor the instructions of the Holy See mention the age which is required of a sister before she may be sent out

---

[19] Mannucci, *loc. cit.*

[20] Decretum "*Singulari quidem,*" 27 mart. 1896—*ASS,* XXVIII (1895-1896), 555–558; *Fontes,* n. 2029. Cf. Schaefer, *De Religiosis,* n. 432; Jorder, "Das Sammeln von Almosen durch Ordensfrauen,"—*AKKR,* (1896), 105-110.

of the convent to solicit alms. Mannucci states that the sister should be at least forty years of age.[21] The Code and the instructions of the Holy See demand that the sisters who are thus commissioned shall be professed, and likewise be of a mature age and mind. It appears that the minimum age requirement, unless specified otherwise in the Constitutions, must for its proper determination be left to the prudent judgment of the superioress. Professed sisters in temporary vows are not necessarily excluded.[22] It may happen in a given community that certain sisters in temporary vows not only are more advanced in years but also more completely formed in character than others who have made their final profession with solemn or perpetual vows.

Finally, canon 623 forbids superioresses to commission for this task sisters who are pursuing studies. It makes no difference whether the studies be sacred or profane, e.g., courses outlined for sisters preparing themselves to become teachers.[23]

For the collecting of alms the sisters are never to be sent out unaccompanied; they shall at all times be sent out in the company of another sister of the community, so that they go in pairs. In this respect the law is more stringent than in the case of religious institutes of men.[24]

In carrying out their task the sisters are to conduct themselves in all modesty, in accordance with their religious profession, carefully shunning all places which may present the slightest danger to themselves or become a source of scandal to the faithful. They are to avoid every semblance of familiarity with men, and to forego all useless conversations. As a further safeguard the Instructions of the Holy See ordain that they enter homes together, and only for a just cause permit themselves to be separated at all.

---

[21] "De Iure et Ratione Quaestuandi," p. 79.

[22] Schaefer, *De Religiosis,* n. 430.

[23] Schaefer, *loc. cit.*

[24] "Superiorissae, praesertim extra locum ubi Domus habent, numquam ad eleemosynas quaerendas mittant Sorores, nisi binas . . ."—Decretum "*Singulari quidem,*" n. 8.

[25] *Decr. cit., loc. cit.*

The superioress shall notify the pastors or other trustworthy persons to whom the local Ordinary has sent letters, so that upon the arrival of the sisters hospitality may be promptly provided at some pious institute of women, or at least with a family whose good repute is beyond suspicion. The sisters shall solicit alms only during the day, and remain at their provided residence while it is dark.[26]

Sisters are not to be absent from their convent longer than a month when collecting in the diocese in which their house is established, or beyond two months when collecting in another diocese.[27] The decree which the Holy See issued with reference to religious sisterhoods does not state that they are to remain in their convent for one month or two months respectively before being sent on a similar mission, a provision which is distinctly stressed for men religious.[28] However, by way of analogy this latter provision embodied in the decree "*De eleemosynis colligendis*" is also applicable to women religious, both sisters and nuns.[29]

Sisters or nuns while on their collection tours shall always carry with them a sufficient amount of money which will enable them to return to their convent immediately upon notice. On their mission they shall perform their spiritual exercises, and if possible assist daily at the Sacrifice of the Mass. During the day they shall solicit alms, not arrogantly as though the offerings were owed, but meekly through a brief explanation of the needs of the religious community. If something is offered let them accept it gratefully; if nothing is offered let them with equal gratitude and patience trust in Divine Providence.[30] They shall carefully adhere to any additional instructions which the religious superioress may issue in the matter. When the allotted time for soliciting has elapsed, they are to return to their convent directly and without delay.[31]

---

[26] *Loc. cit.*

[27] *Loc. cit.*

[28] Decretum, "*De eleemosynis colligendis,*" I, 10.

[29] Cf. canon 490.

[30] Decretum "*Singulari quidem,*" n. 8.

[31] *Loc. cit.*

Article 3

JURISDICTIONAL CONTROL BY LOCAL ORDINARIES OVER ALMS-GATHERING BY RELIGIOUS

In order properly to evaluate the jurisdictional control which local Ordinaries possess over alms-gathering by religious, it is important and necessary to consider first the degree of exemption which certain religious enjoy, and then the extent of control which local Ordinaries have in the exercise of jurisdiction. By jurisdiction is here understood the *iurisdictio regiminis,* which implies not merely legislative power, or the power of making laws, of imposing precepts and of applying penalties legitimately decreed, but also that of attaching penalties to a law or precept.[32]

Regulars, whether men [33] or women,[34] with the exception of nuns who are not subject to regular superiors, are exempt from the jurisdiction of the local Ordinary unless the contrary is expressly stated in the law.[35] All other religious, unless they enjoy exemption similar to regulars by reason of their Constitutions or through a special Indult, are subject to the local Ordinary according to the norms of law.[36]

The legislation of local Ordinaries, enacted by them either individually or collectively, does not affect religious in those matters in which they are exempt. If religious are exempted from the jurisdiction of local Ordinaries, they are also exempted from their primary act of jurisdiction, which is that of enacting laws.[37] Thus neither plenary nor provincial Councils, nor diocesan synods, can enact laws on alms-gathering which are contrary to the exemptive rights and privileges which religious possess in ac-

---

[32] Canon 2220, § 1; O'Brien, *Exemption of Religious in Church Law,* p. 23; Wernz-Vidal, *Ius Canonicum,* II, n. 48.

[33] Canon 487, n. 7.

[34] Canon 487, n. 7, together with canon 500, § 2.

[35] Canons 615 and 500, § 2.

[36] "Subduntur quoque religiosi Ordinario loci, iis exceptis qui a Sede Apostolica exemptionis privilegium consecuti sunt, salva semper potestate quam ius etiam in eos locorum Ordinariis concedit."—Canon 500, § 1.

[37] O'Brien, *Exemption of Religious in Church Law,* p. 34.

cordance with the provision of law or the grant of a particular privilege.[38]

In so far as religious are exempt from the legislative power of local Ordinaries, they are in virtue of that same exemption immune from the coercive jurisdiction of local Ordinaries.[39] However, in all matters in which religious are subject to local Ordinaries, they may be coerced even with penalties according to canon 619.[40] The term "religious" (*religiosi*) in canon 619 includes regulars in those instances in which they do not enjoy exemption.[41]

With these general principles in mind, one can more readily undertake to make an analysis of the control by local Ordinaries in the matter of alms-gathering by religious.

Mendicants who are such in name and in fact[42] can with the sole permission of their superiors collect alms in the diocese in which their house is situated.[43] In virtue of this exemption such mendicants, as well as other religious who enjoy a similar privilege by reason of their Constitutions or through an apostolic Indult, can in no manner be restricted by local Ordinaries, either individually by means of particular diocesan laws, or collectively by means of the decrees of provincial or plenary Councils, as long as they collect alms in the diocese in which the religious house is canonically established.

Even if, for instance, any of the above-mentioned religious should commit transgressions while on such a mission, local Ordinaries cannot withdraw the privilege, impose remedial legislation on them without a special sanction from the Holy See, or punish them except under certain conditions, as will be noted later on.

---

[38] Cf. C. 17, X, *de excessibus praelatorum,* V, 31; Benedictus XIV, *De Synodo Dioecesana* (Venetiis, 1795), L. IX, c. 15: O'Brien, *loc. cit.*

[39] Cf. O'Brien, *op. cit.*, pp. 48–50.

[40] "In omnibus in quibus religiosi subsunt Ordinario loci, possunt ab eodem etiam poenis coerceri."—Canon 619. Cf. canon 2220, § 1.

[41] Scheuermann, *Die Exemption nach geltendem Kirchlichen Recht,* Görres-Gesellschaft Veröffentlichungen der Sektion für Rechts—und Staatswissenschaft, 77. Heft (Paderborn: Schöningh, 1938), pp. 130–132 (Hereafter cited as *Exemption*).

[42] Cf. P.C.I., 16 oct. 1919—*AAS,* XI (1919), 478.

[43] Canon 621, § 1.

The following religious, however, are subject to local Ordinaries in the soliciting of alms in so far as local Ordinaries have control over its exercise, namely, in granting or in denying the permission (*licentia*) spoken of in canon 621, § 2, and canon 622:

1. Mendicants in the strict sense and other religious who enjoy a similar privilege, but only when they solicit alms outside the diocese in which their religious house is established.

2. All regulars, even though otherwise exempt, if they do not enjoy the privilege of the mendicants in the strict sense.

3. All religious of congregations of pontifical approval who do not share in the above-mentioned privilege of mendicants in virtue of their Constitutions or by special apostolic Indult, and all religious of diocesan institutes.

Any regulations which a local Ordinary in granting the permission for the collecting of alms may impose by way of a personal precept or by means of a particular law are mandatory as long as they do not run counter to the law of the Code. Commands and injunctions may be enforced even with punitive measures.

When permission is required for the soliciting of alms, the local Ordinary may of course for justifiable reasons withdraw his previously granted permission. Violations of particular regulations, e.g., with reference to the allotted time or the designated territory, would constitute a sufficient reason for such a withdrawal. In withdrawing his permission the local Ordinary of a diocese other than that in which religious mendicants have a canonically established house *ipso facto* restricts the right of exercising the privilege of collecting alms.[44]

Apart from the control which a local Ordinary enjoys in regard to the exercise of the privilege of soliciting alms, the Code provides other relevant coercive measures, a consideration of which is appropriate at this point.

Exempt religious unlawfully dwelling outside their convent, even under the pretext of having recourse to their superior, do not enjoy the privilege of exemption.[45] When such religious unlawfully dwelling outside their convent solicit alms or are guilty

---

[44] Cf. canons 621 and 622, § 1.

[45] Canon 616, § 1. Cf. canons 601; 606; 607; 644, § 3; 684, §§ 1–2.

of other excesses they are to be punished according to the gravity of their offense by the local Ordinary in virtue of canon 619. In such an instance their status is the same as that of non-exempt religious. Juridically the local Ordinary has such punitive power also over mendicants who are such in the strict sense if they dwell unlawfully outside their religious house and solicit alms, even in the diocese in which their convent is established.

Regulars who have committed a crime outside their house, and are not punished by their superior after he has been informed of the transgression, may be punished by the local Ordinary even though they may have legitimately left their house and returned to it.[46] Thus if regulars commit a crime, or occasion a scandal for the faithful, or even against legitimate prohibition dare to solicit alms, the local Ordinary can demand that such religious return to their house, and request the superior to punish them according to the gravity of their offense. If the religious superior fails to heed the admonition, such delinquent regulars can be punished by the local Ordinary himself.[47] The power of the local Ordinary in this instance is conditional. He cannot punish them if the religious superior, when duly admonished, takes punitive measures.[48]

Institutes with simple vows do not enjoy the privilege of exemption unless it has been specifically conceded to them.[49] The local Ordinary can without limitation withdraw from them the permission of soliciting alms in his diocese, and punish violations of his admonitions with suitable penalties.[50]

---

[46] Canon 616, § 2.

[47] Cf. Schaefer, *De Religiosis*, n. 421; Fanfani, *De Iure Religiosorum*, n. 353; Coronata, *Compendium Iuris Canonici*, I, n. 1095.

[48] O'Brien, *Exemption of Religious in Church Law*, p. 51.

[49] Canon 618, § 1.

[50] Cf. canons 619; 2220, § 1.

CHAPTER VII

ALMS-GATHERING BY ORIENTALS

ARTICLE 1

ORIENTALS AND CANON 622, § 4

Canon 622, § 4: Sine authentico et recenti rescripto Sacrae Congregationis pro Ecclesia Orientali, Ordinarii latini nec sinant orientalem ullum cuiusvis ordinis et dignitatis in proprio territorio pecuniam colligere, nec suum subditum in orientales dioeceses ad eundem finem mittant.

(a) *General Notions*

Canon 1 explains the relation of the Latin Code towards Oriental discipline. The Code of Canon Law, though it frequently has reference to the discipline of the Oriental Church, nevertheless concerns the Latin Church only and does not obligate the Oriental, unless it is treating of those matters which from the very nature of the case affect also the Oriental.[1]

This norm of action is based upon a decree of the Sacred Congregation of the Propagation of the Faith of November 8, 1882,[2] wherein the Sacred Congregation determined that the constitutions of the Holy See are binding upon the Oriental Church in the following cases:

(a) if they concern matters of faith and Catholic doctrine;

(b) if their subject matter shows that they are binding upon Orientals for the reason that they are not merely ecclesiastical laws, but also declarations of the divine or natural law;

(c) if the laws themselves, though disciplinary in character, expressly include Orientals.[3]

[1] Canon 1.

[2] *Collectanea,* n. 1578; *Fontes,* n. 4899.

[3] Cicognani, *Commentarium ad Librum I Codicis* (Romae: Ex Schola Typographica "Pio X," 1925), p. 9.

Canon 622, § 4, belongs to the last category just enumerated, inasmuch as it is disciplinary in character and expressly embraces Oriental Catholics. It states that Orientals of whatever order or dignity must have an authentic and recent rescript from the Sacred Congregation for the Oriental Church, before the Ordinaries of the Latin rite may permit them to collect alms in their territory. Canon 622, § 4, furthermore provides that Latin Ordinaries must obtain a similar rescript from the Sacred Congregation to send their subjects to Oriental dioceses for a similar purpose.

The legislation of the Code may be considered a dispositive arrangement of previous constitutions, decrees, and letters emanating from the Holy See,[4] and as a nucleus of the declarations and instructions issued by the Sacred Congregation for the Oriental Church since the promulgation of the Code of Canon Law in 1918.[5] With these sources in mind one can readily institute an analysis and an interpretation of canon 622, § 4.

(*b*) *Canon 622, § 4*

By Orientals in canon 622, § 4, are meant not merely religious but all Catholics who belong to an Oriental rite, regardless of where they may have their residence or affiliation in a certain rite.[6] This legislation binds them wherever they are, be that in the Orient, in Europe, or in America.[7]

---

[4] Innocentius XI, decretum "*Cum sancta,*" 4 febr. 1677—*Bullarium Pontificium S. Congregationis de Propaganda Fide,* I, 229; Alexander VIII, const. "*Alias emanavit,*" 21 oct. 1690—*BRT,* XX, 145; Clemens XII, const. "*Dudum emanavit,*" 26 mart. 1736—*BRT,* XXIV, 163; S.C. de Prop. Fide, litt. encycl. 24 sept. 1882—*Collectanea,* n. 1575; *Fontes,* n. 4898; S.C. de Prop. Fide, ep. circular. 12 apr. 1894—*Collectanea,* n. 1866; S.C. de Prop. Fide, ep. circular. 1 ian. 1912—*AAS,* IV (1912), 532-533; *Fontes,* n. 4942.

[5] Monitum "*Praecavens abusus mendicantium,*" 2 apr. 1928—*AAS,* XX (1928), 107; decretum "*Qua sollerti,*" 23 dec. 1929—*AAS,* XXII (1930), 99; decretum "*Non raro accidit,*" 2 ian. 1930—*AAS,* XXII (1930), 106; decretum "*Saepenumero,*" 7 ian. 1930—*AAS,* XXII (1930), 108; decretum "*Quo facilior,*" 26 sept. 1932—*AAS,* XXIV (1932), 344; monitum "*Sacrae Congregationi,*" 20 iul. 1937—*AAS,* XXIX (1937), 342.

[6] Dausend, *Das interrituelle Recht im Codex Iuris Canonici,* Görres-Gesellschaft, Veröffentlichungen der Sektion für Rechts—und Staatswissenschaft, 79. Heft (Paderborn: Schöningh, 1939), p. 110; Schaefer, *De*

This is also stated by the Sacred Congregation for the Oriental Church in its decree "*Qua solerti*" of January 7, 1930, which regards Oriental clerics, secular or religious, who go from Oriental territories or dioceses to North, Central, or South America, or to Australia, to minister spiritually to the faithful of their own rite in those places. All priests who go there for the aforesaid purpose are forbidden to collect alms without permission from this Sacred Congregation.[8] It seems that this provision of canon 622, § 4, also includes persons who are born in Europe or America and have been affiliated with an Oriental rite through baptism, on the occasion of marriage, or in consequence of a rescript of the Apostolic See.[9]

"Cuiusvis ordinis et dignitatis." A few authors give an interpretation of this passage. Duskie[10] restricts the scope of canon 622, § 4, to religious of the Oriental rite, and contends that other Oriental collectors are bound only by similar legislation in decrees enacted by the Sacred Congregation of the Propagation of the Faith.[11]

Dausend,[12] Schaefer,[13] and Augustine[14] include not merely religious but all Orientals, be they laymen or clerics, even bishops and patriarchs.

The view expressed by Dausend, Schaefer, and Augustine seems not only an acceptable but also the tenable opinion. In support of it the following reasons may be advanced:

1. The terminology "*Ordinarii latini nec sinant Orientalem ullum*" is an expression of its very nature general and not specific. Its universality of concept is emphasized by the phrase "*cuiusvis ordinis et dignitatis,*" which includes all persons of

---

Religiosis, n. 431; Vermeersch-Creusen, *Epitome Iuris Canonici,* I, n. 68 sub d.

[7] Schaefer, *De Religiosis,* n. 431. Other authors available do not express an opinion on this particular point.

[8] Art. 16—*AAS,* XXII (1930), 104.

[9] Cf. canons 98, 756.

[10] *The Canonical Status of the Orientals in the United States,* p. 108.

[11] Fanfani (*De Iure Religiosorum,* n. 358) seems to hold a similar view.

[12] *Das interrituelle Recht im Codex Iuris Canonici,* p. 110.

[13] *De Religiosis,* n. 431.

[14] *A Commentary on the New Code of Canon Law,* III, 349.

whatever rank and dignity. The word "*ordo*" in this context cannot be taken in the restrictive sense of "*ordo*" as defined in canon 488, n. 2.[15]

2. The terms, *regulares, religiosi,* are not embodied as restrictive words in this particular paragraph of the canon. On the contrary, all other portions of canon 622 as well as other canons [16] which govern alms-gathering by religious, are through the employment of such terms restricted in their application so as to point exclusively to members of religious institutes.

3. The decree of Innocent XI of February 4, 1677,[17] which forbade all Greek Orientals to collect alms, definitely referred to *seculars* as well as to ecclesiastics including *regulars.* The subsequent constitutions of Alexander VIII [18] and Clement XII [19] which forbade the collecting of alms by Orientals, restated and reaffirmed the decree of Innocent XI.

4. Decrees which previous and subsequent to the legislation of the Code of Canon Law forbade Oriental clerics to collect alms or Mass stipends without special authorization from the Holy See make no distinction as to their state of life or their rank, and are held to be obligatory for both seculars and religious.

5. The decree of the Sacred Congregation for the Oriental Church "*Saepenumero,*" [20] which forbids Oriental clerics without the special permission of the Sacred Congregation for the Oriental Church to collect money or Mass stipends, expressly repeats and recalls to mind the provision of canon 622, § 4.

Orientals do not come under the provision of canon 1503, which forbids the collecting of alms for pious and ecclesiastical purposes by all private persons, whether lay or clerical, without the authorization of the Holy See or of their own proper Ordinary and the permission of the Ordinary of the place in which they wish to solicit. This canon is disciplinary in character, and no mention

---

[15] Dausend, *Das interrituelle Recht im Codex Iuris Canonici,* p. 111.

[16] Canons 621; 623; 624; 630, § 4.

[17] *Bullarium Pontificium S. Cong. de Prop. Fide,* I, 229.

[18] "*Alias emanavit,*" 21 oct. 1690—*BRT,* XX, 145.

[19] "*Dudum emanavit,*" 26 mart. 1736—*BRT,* XXIV, 163.

[20] 7 ian. 1930—*AAS,* XXII (1930), 108.

is made of Orientals directly or indirectly; hence it is obligatory only for Catholics of the Latin Church.[21]

Seculars and religious who belong to the Latin rite, however, do not need the special authorization of the Sacred Congregation for the Oriental Church to collect alms for the benefit of pious and ecclesiastical purposes in Oriental territories as long as they remain in territory of the Latin rite.[22]

Oriental priests subject to Latin Ordinaries, or to Ordinaries of their own rite, are not forbidden to collect alms for purposes intended for the spiritual benefit of the people of their jurisdiction. In this case Oriental priests act as pastors and rectors in an official capacity, and not as private persons.[23] However, if such Oriental pastors or rectors solicit outside their territory, or within it for purposes foreign to that of their specific charge, they no longer act in an official capacity, but rather as private persons, and consequently they must obtain the necessary authorization from the Sacred Congregation for the Oriental Church and observe all local regulations.[24]

"Pecuniam colligere." Canon 622, § 4, does not distinguish the method of collecting money which is prohibited by it. Certainly personal collections are meant, since they are more easily marked by indiscreet conduct than written petitions in letters and periodicals, wherein the usefulness and the necessity of pious and charitable undertakings may be conservatively described.

Of itself the terminology "*pecuniam colligere*" does not include the collecting of Mass stipends and other alms besides money.[25] As far as Mass stipends are concerned canon 838 provides at least indirectly: Persons who have a number of manual stipends which they are at liberty to give to others, may distribute them among priests of their own choice (including priests of the Oriental rite), provided that they know for certain that the lat-

---

[21] Cf. canon 1.

[22] Schaefer, *De Religiosis*, n. 431.

[23] Doheny, *Church Property: Modes of Acquisition*, p. 51; Duskie, *The Canonical Status of the Orientals in the United States*, p. 108.

[24] Doheny, *loc. cit.;* Duskie, *loc. cit.*

[25] Schaefer, *De Religiosis*, n. 431.

ter are absolutely trustworthy, or are recommended by the testimony of their own Ordinaries.

The collecting of Mass stipends by Orientals in a Latin diocese is expressly mentioned as forbidden in the decree "*Saepenumero*" of the Sacred Congregation for the Oriental Church.[26] Article 1 of this decree reads: In order that any collection, whether of money or of Mass stipends, be made in a Latin diocese by an Oriental cleric of whatsoever order or dignity, the permission of the Sacred Congregation for the Oriental Church is absolutely required.[27] In article 2 and article 3 of this same decree the Sacred Congregation further states that it does not make it a practice to grant permission to collect either money or Mass stipends. Only in extraordinary circumstances will permission be granted, and then local Ordinates will be notified in advance directly or indirectly through an Apostolic nuncio or delegate.

"Sine authentico et recenti rescripto Sacrae Congregationis pro Ecclesia Orientali." The rescript permitting Orientals to collect alms must originate from the Sacred Congregation for the Oriental Church. To this Sacred Congregation, of which the Roman Pontiff is the Prefect, are reserved all affairs of every kind relating to persons, discipline, and rites of the Oriental Church, with due regard to the jurisdiction necessarily reserved to the Holy Office.[28] Russians, whether in Russia or out of it, can now obtain a similar rescript from the Commission for Russia.[29] The Commission for Russia, instituted in 1925 and formerly joined to the Sacred Congregation for the Oriental Church,[30] was separated from the Sacred Congregation by a *motu proprio* of Pius XI on April 6, 1930, and constituted *sui iuris*.[31]

The rescript issuing from either of the two above-mentioned sources must be recent. Certainly if the time allotted in the rescript has expired, the collections must cease, and the local Ordi-

---

[26] 7 ian. 1930—*AAS*, XXII (1930), 108.

[27] Translation from Bouscaren, *The Canon Law Digest*, I, 27.

[28] Cf. canons 247, 257.

[29] Vermeersch-Creusen, *Epitome Iuris Canonici*, I, n. 782.

[30] *AAS*, XVIII (1926), 62.

[31] *AAS*, XXII (1930), 153.

nary cannot permit Orientals to continue collecting money and Mass stipends before a new rescript has been obtained. If no definite time is indicated in the rescript, the rescript could scarcely be considered recent if it is a year old, and hence would be intrinsically subject to suspicion.[32]

The rescript must be authentic; its authenticity can be ascertained from the date and seal affixed by the Sacred Congregation for the Oriental Church or by the Commission for Russia. Deception in this matter is not easily possible, since advance information about the identity of the collectors and the concession, in virtue of the decree *Saepenumero,* is to be sent henceforth directly by the Holy See or through a Legate of the Roman Pontiff to the local Ordinaries. Without this advance information local Ordinaries are forbidden to permit collectors to solicit money or Mass stipends, even though they possess letters and documents from other Ordinaries or from any ecclesiastical dignitaries, or even though they present documents purporting their issuance from the Sacred Congregation for the Oriental Church.[33]

Canon 622, § 4, also forbids Latin Ordinaries to send any of their subjects into Oriental dioceses for similar collections of money. By Latin Ordinaries are here understood not merely local Ordinaries, but also major religious superiors of exempt clerical institutes.[34] If for special reasons [35] Latin Ordinaries deem it necessary to send their subjects into Oriental dioceses, then the permission must be sought from the Sacred Congregation for the Oriental Church or from the Commission for Russia.[36]

---

[32] Schaefer, *De Religiosis,* n. 431; Vermeersch-Creusen, *Epitome Iuris Canonici,* n. 782; Augustine (*A Commentary on the New Code of Canon Law,* III, 349) considers a rescript recent only within six months after its concession.

[33] Decretum *"Saepenumero,"* art. 4—*AAS,* XXII (1930), 108.

[34] Canon 198, § 1.

[35] "Posterior casus vix unquam eveniet. Dispositio tamen istud commodum habet parcendi Orientalium nomini. Si Latinis liceret apud Orientales quod his apud Latinos vetatur, sanctio nimis odiosa videretur, et suspicionem in Orientales iniiceret."—Vermeersch-Creusen, *Epitome Iuris Canonici,* I, n. 782.

[36] Canon 257, § 1.

In the United States of America the decree of the III Plenary Council of Baltimore (1884) must be recognized. This Council decreed that priests, secular and religious, who come from abroad without proper authorization to collect alms are not to be permitted to say Mass, not even once, without the permission of the local Ordinary.[37]

This decree of the Council of Baltimore includes all clerical collectors from abroad. Since it makes no exceptions it is binding also on Oriental priests.[38] The decree, in being a particular law which is not contrary to the Code of Canon Law, is still effective.[39] Then, too, canon 804, § 3, prescribes that all particular norms enacted by the local Ordinary relative to the admission of extra-diocesan priests to the celebration of Mass must be observed. This provision seems adequate endorsement of the conciliar decree.

ARTICLE 2

Monita AND DECREES SINCE THE PROMULGATION OF THE CODE OF CANON LAW

Since the promulgation of the Code of Canon Law frequent reports of abuses among Oriental alms-collectors have been reported to the Holy See. Abuses were reported not merely among Oriental clerics, but also among certain Oriental laymen who, as the *monitum "Sacrae Congregationi"* of the Sacred Congregation for the Oriental Church of July 20, 1937, indicates,[40] fraudulently exhibited false credentials, used the name and dress of Oriental priests, and thus wandered through various lands, beg-

---

[37] *Acta et Decreta Concilii Plenarii Baltimorensis Tertii,* n. 295. This decree is not to be understood for religious saying Mass privately in the monasteries of their own order.—*Acta et Decreta,* n. 295.

[38] Duskie, *The Canonical Status of the Orientals in the United States,* p. 108. Duskie maintains, and rightly so, that Orientals are themselves obliged to the observance of the Baltimore decree. Violation of this decree would result in abuses and scandal to the great detriment of the faithful and of the welfare of the Church in general. It was precisely for this reason that the decree was enacted.

[39] Canon 6, n. 1.

[40] *AAS,* XXIX (1937), 342.

ging alms, collecting Mass stipends, and even demanding the right to celebrate the Sacrifice of the Mass.

The Sacred Congregation for the Oriental Church in this *monitum "Sacrae Congregationi"* urgently entreats local Ordinaries to remember the regulations and decrees which have been promulgated and to strive through their application completely to eradicate any further impositions and wrongs of this kind. For this reason all the decrees and *monita* of the Sacred Congregation for the Oriental Church in reference to collecting alms, money, and Mass stipends are here set forth in their relevant paragraphs.

1. *Monitum—"Praecavens abusus mendicantium,"* of April 2, 1928[41]

The *monitum "Praecavens abusus mendicantium"* of the Sacred Congregation for the Oriental Church reads as follows:

> It has often been reported to the Sacred Oriental Congregation that certain persons who claim to be Orientals, or even, under a false name, claim to belong to the Oriental clergy, wander about through the dioceses of Italy and of foreign countries, collecting money or asking for Mass stipends.
>
> These impostors, in order the more easily to deceive, usually present writings and documents, sometimes even photographs, which they say have been given them by prelates, but which are found to be either false or given for another purpose.
>
> Accordingly, the Sacred Congregation declares and gives notice that no one has permission to beg money or to collect Mass stipends; and in order to hold in check such great audacity and especially to protect the dignity and good repute of the Orientals, especially of Oriental priests, it once more urgently requests the Ordinaries of places to be on their guard lest pastors, Superiors of religious houses, and the faithful themselves, be deceived by these collectors of money; and to see that they do not receive these persons, and much less give them Masses to

---

[41] S.C. pro Eccl. Or.—*AAS,* XX (1928), 107; Bouscaren, *The Canon Law Digest,* I, 6. The translations of the *Monita* and Decrees of the Sacred Oriental Congregation in this Article are taken from this author's cited work.

be said, the latter being a grave obligation in conscience as regards the celebration of the Masses.

2. Decree—"*Cum data fuerit,*" of March 1, 1929[42]

The decree "*Cum data fuerit*" of the Sacred Congregation for the Oriental Church, regarding the spiritual administration of the Greek-Ruthenians in the United States, has the following in Chapter II, Article 13:

> Priests who are looking for money, or who are vacillating in faith and morals, or who are given to drink, shall by no means be sent to America, nor allowed to come there; and if any such are found, let them be sent away as quickly as possible. If, when they have been sent away, they fail to obey, let them be coerced with canonical penalties, including suspension from sacred functions.

3. Decree—"*Qua sollerti*" of December 23, 1929[43]

The decree "*Qua sollerti*" of the Sacred Congregation for the Oriental Church regarding Oriental clerics, secular or religious, who go from Oriental territories or dioceses to North, Central, or South America, or to Australia, to minister spiritually to the faithful of their own rite in those places, states the following:

> With what alert readiness the Apostolic See has at all time provided for the eternal salvation of those faithful of the Oriental rites who have gone from the Patriarchal territories, countries, and dioceses of the Oriental rite, to foreign shores, especially in cases where they established a domicile there, the many documents and decrees which have been issued on this subject clearly testify.
>
> For Holy Mother Church has had nothing more at heart than to strive with all solicitude that, amid so many dangers which arise especially in those foreign countries, particularly from their contact and intercourse with heretical sects and schismatics of the Oriental rite, these faithful also should keep their Catholic faith intact and

---

[42] S.C. pro Eccl. Or.—*AAS,* XXI (1929), 152–159; Bouscaren, *The Canon Law Digest,* I, 6–16.

[43] S.C. pro Eccl. Or.—*AAS,* XXII (1930), 99–105; Bouscaren, *The Canon Law Digest,* I, 17–24.

inviolate; and that they should be able to use freely their own Oriental rite, even when they lived among Catholics of the Latin rite. Wherefore the Church was also ever desirous that for the spiritual care of these emigrants, priests of the Oriental rite should be chosen from the Patriarchal or Oriental territories, who, being possessed of learning and of good moral character, should be qualified for this most sacred ministry, and who could confidently be sent to minister spiritually to the faithful of their own rite. For the same reason it was provided that the outstanding qualities of these priests should be recognized in advance, and that the Ordinaries of places to which they wished to go should not only be willing to receive them but should await them as welcome companions in the labors of the Lord's vineyard. And to this end appropriate laws and decrees have very often been enacted by the Holy See.

But, since in the course of time these laws and decrees have either not been well understood or have passed, as it were, into oblivion, and not a few abuses have arisen of such a nature as to be likely to cause serious detriment to good priests of the Oriental rite, this Sacred Congregation has deemed it opportune and even necessary to mention those laws and decrees once more and to restore them, especially for the purpose of providing more effectively for the spiritual welfare of the faithful of the Oriental rite. For, as has frequently been reported to this Sacred Congregation, certain priests, espesially from among those who have gone to America and Australia, have on account of their conduct merited serious criticism and, as it were, a note of censure, not merely from the faithful of the Latin rite, but even from their own of the Oriental rite. Others, seeking their own interest and not that of Jesus Christ, have basely abandoned the faithful entrusted to their care and have gone wandering about. Others still, who were not even Catholics or in sacred orders, have so shrewdly deceived the Ordinaries of places by means of forged testimonials, that the latter sometimes complained that it was almost if not quite impossible to distinguish good priests from bad, and legitimate ones from impostors and liars. Such being the case, no one will fail to see how seriously the excellent priests of the Oriental rite are handicapped in their work, and hence how necessary it is to apply suitable remedies to the situation without delay.

Yet in seeking these remedies, this Sacred Congregation felt that it was not necessary to change the laws and decrees which have often been enacted by the Holy See, but that it would be better to restore and renew them, and at the same time to provide a certain and definite method by which these laws and decrees might be more swiftly and more perfectly applied, and opportunities for evading them might be precluded.

Surely this Sacred Congregation need not hesitate to recommend to the Latin Bishops of those countries the Orientals who live in their dioceses; for the Sacred Congregation is well aware of the great charity which, especially in these times, is being shown not only by the Latin Bishops but by Apostolic Nuntios and Delegates toward the Orientals, even toward those who are separated from the unity of the Church; for more than one schismatical community or parish has been brought back to the unity of the Church through the care and industry of the Bishops of America.

Those Ordinaries are therefore more and more earnestly requested to apply themselves with all zeal, earnestness, and industry, especially according to the Constitution, *Orientalium dignitas,* n. IX,[44] to the care of the Orientals who live in their dioceses, so as to try to provide, as far as possible, churches and even schools for them without interfering with their rite. If they cannot under the circumstances have schools of their own, the Ordinaries shall at least make every effort that these Orientals be not, as it were, forced to send their children to Protestant schools, or to schools foreign to the spirit of Christ. Also and especially they should foster ecclesiastical vocations in the native-born children of those faithful of the Oriental rite, and see that they be not only trained to piety and instructed in ecclesiastical studies, but also, after consulting this Sacred Congregation, that they be duly instructed in their own rite, and ordained. For if they too are thus trained and instructed, and are applied to the spiritual care of the faithful of their own rite, fuller provision will have been made for this spiritual work, since their services will be more fittingly rendered and more readily accepted.

In order, therefore, that it may better protect the reputation of Oriental priests, and at the same time provide for the spiritual care of the faithful of the Oriental rite, after full discussion of the matter at the general session

---

[44] *Fontes,* n. 627.

of the Eminent Fathers held on 17 June, 1929, this Sacred Congregation provides and decrees as follows regarding Oriental priests who go to America or Australia to exercise the pastoral ministry there; and these provisions are to be carefully and faithfully observed, not only by the Ordinaries and priests of the Oriental rite, but also, in virtue of canon 257, by the Ordinaries of the Latin rite.

1. The Ordinaries of places who belong to the Latin rite, as above mentioned, shall learn whether any Catholics of the Oriental rite have moved into or are residing in their dioceses; to what certain and definite Oriental rite they belong, and whether they are in need of spiritual ministrations from a priest of their own rite; and if so, they shall without delay signify and declare the existing need or advantage of such spiritual care, to this Sacred Congregation, through the Apostolic Nuntio or Delegate of the country, who shall if necessary investigate and approve the aforesaid need or advantage.

2. If the Lord Patriarchs or Oriental Bishops be in any way notified of this advantage or necessity of spiritual care from priests of their own rite for the faithful of the Oriental rite in those places, they shall likewise make it known to this Sacred Congregation, at the same time indicating the diocese or dioceses where the faithful in question are living, and designating or proposing some worthy and suitable priest or priests as above indicated. This notice shall be sent through the Apostolic Nuntio or Delegate, who shall give his opinion, as above indicated, regarding the priests whose names are proposed.

This Sacred Congregation will immediately give notice of the matter to the Bishop of the place above mentioned, through the Apostolic Nuntio or Delegate, and will at the same time ask the opinion of the Apostolic Delegate or Nuntio on the whole matter.

3. If any of the faithful desire the spiritual ministration of a priest of their own rite, it will be better to ask for them of the Ordinary of the place, who shall send the request, together with his own recommendation or consent, to the Apostolic Delegate or Nuntio of the country, who shall forward it to this Sacred Congregation with his questions, information, and recommendation.

4. Indeed, not only the Lord Patriarchs and the Ordinaries either of the Oriental or of the Latin rite, but

also the faithful may directly communicate these matters to this Sacred Congregation; but not a little time will be saved if the thing is done in the way above indicated.

5. The Oriental Bishop or Bishops, or Patriarch, when designating, as above outlined in Articles 1 and 2, some worthy and suitable priest or priests for spiritual ministry, shall at the same time send on testimonial letters for the celebration of Mass, and inform the Sacred Congregation of his or their past record and character, and of whatever may serve to prove him or them worthy and qualified for the task to be assigned them.

If there is question of a priest of the regular clergy, his selection and the information regarding him shall be sent also by his Superior.

6. Secular priests who have a wife shall not be admitted to exercise the sacred ministry in these countries, but only celibate priests or widowers. Widowers may, however, for just cause, be excluded by this Sacred Congregation from those dioceses and places in which they may have children living or in any way present; and the same is true of the adjoining localities.

7. As soon as this Sacred Congregation, upon receiving the required information, shall have approved the priest who has been designated, it will, by special rescript in the usual way, grant the permission for the said priest to go to a certain diocese, establish his domicile there, and give spiritual aid to the faithful of his own race or rite.

In order to avoid all doubt or difficulty on the part of the Bishops of these countries, this Sacred Congregation will send the aforesaid rescript or permission to the Ordinary of the diocese where the priest of the Oriental rite intends to establish his domicile, through the Apostolic Nuntio or Delegate or, if the matter is urgent, directly to the Ordinary, giving notice at the same time to the Apostolic Nuntio or Delegate. The granting of this permission shall belong exclusively to this Sacred Congregation, to the exclusion of the Ordinaries, and even of the Patriarchs; and the Sacred Congregation will grant the permission only in writing or by rescript.

8. The Sacred Congregation will send the permission to the priest who has been designated, either through the Apostolic Nuntio or Delegate, or, with notice to him, through the proper Ordinary, or, as above stated, through the Patriarch; and if there is question of a religious priest, through his Superior, with notice to the

Apostolic Delegate, and if need be, to the Patriarch. And together with the permission it will send to the same priest in the manner above described, testimonial letters commonly called a *celebret,* which shall be valid for the purpose stated, and for the time required for the journey.

9. The priest shall without delay, as soon as he can, proceed to the designated place. If it is necessary to interrupt the journey for a time, the priest may be admitted to say Mass, upon presenting to the rector of the church where he wishes to say it the testimonial letters or *celebret* which he has received from the Sacred Oriental Congregation. The rector shall enter upon the *celebret* a notation of the date when Mass was celebrated, together with the title of the church, and his own signature.

If the said priest of the Oriental rite tarries longer than is proper, the rector of the church shall inform the Bishop or Ordinary of the place of that fact. The Ordinary shall refuse further permission to celebrate Mass to those priests who, without just cause, tarry too long at any point along the way, or gad about; and, without prejudice to his own right in the premises, shall moreover report the matter to the Apostolic Nuntio or Delegate, or to this Sacred Congregation.

10. As soon as the aforesaid priest arrives at the designated diocese, he shall present himself to the Ordinary of the place, and show him the testimonial letters which he has from the Sacred Congregation, and the discessorial letters from his own Bishop or from the Lord Patriarch.

The Ordinary of the place, in accordance with the rescript from this Sacred Congregation which is mentioned in Article 7, shall give the priest permission to celebrate Mass or the divine Liturgy, to administer the sacraments, and to perform all sacred functions, as well as to take up headquarters for the spiritual care of the faithful of his own rite, and whatever else is necessary and helpful; he shall also assign him a place in which he is to establish his domicile.

11. The priest shall be subject to the jurisdiction of the Ordinary of the place.

12. Hence, always without prejudice to his own rite, he must obey the orders of the Ordinary of the place, both as regards the spiritual care of his faithful in the church and place assigned to him, and as regards going

to any other church, parish, or place within the diocese to exercise his ministry, or to visit the faithful of his rite in the course of his sacred ministry.

Nor may he go to another diocese for the temporary exercise of his sacred ministry or to visit the faithful of his own rite, unless with the previous consent of both the Bishop *a quo* and the Bishop *ad quem;* and if he has this consent, he must behave in the manner and according to the method and conditions laid down by the aforesaid Superiors.

13. In order that a priest, who has gone to any diocese of America or Australia, may change from one diocese to another within those countries, it is enough that the Bishop *a quo* and the Bishop *ad quem* agree on the matter, each signifying his consent in writing. The Bishop *ad quem* is obliged to send notice of the matter as soon as possible, through the Apostolic Nuntio or Delegate, to the Sacred Oriental Congregation.

14. At the end of every year, counting from the date of the rescript, every Oriental priest who is living in these countries is obliged to send to the Sacred Oriental Congregation a written report of the religious state of his people, and of his fulfillment of his sacred ministry. He shall show this report to the Ordinary of the place, so that the latter may authoritatively approve it in writing, adding, as he judges opportune, his own annotations thereto. The Ordinary himself will send the report to this Sacred Congregation.

15. Let no Bishop, therefore, admit to this diocese any priest of the Oriental rite coming from an Oriental diocese, and grant him the permission of celebrating Mass or of exercising the sacred ministry, unless he has received beforehand the necessary rescript from the Sacred Oriental Congregation according to Article 7. Likewise, unless he has received this rescript, to prevent all fraud, let no Ordinary give credit to any letters or documents, even purporting to come from this Sacred Congregation, which may be presented by a priest or by one claiming to be a priest; and, without prejudice to his own right in the premises, let the Ordinary in such case refer the matter to the Apostolic Nuntio or Delegate of his country, or to this Sacred Congregation.

In the meantime the Ordinary of the place may, according to his prudent judgment, through the remedies and sanctions outlined in Article 9, attend to any Oriental priest who, for the purpose aforesaid, has come into his diocese without the required permission.

16. All priests who, for the aforesaid purpose, remain there (without prejudice to the prohibition against collecting alms or money without permission from this Sacred Congregation), shall, as regards the stipends of Masses and the usual offerings which are made according to the custom of the diocese for divine worship and for the support of churches and schools, abide absolutely by the diocesan regulations and decrees; unless in particular cases the Ordinary sees fit to provide otherwise for them.

17. The provisions of Articles 11, 12, 13, 14, 15, and 16 apply also to those Oriental priests who went to those countries before the publication of this Decree, and who are lawfully staying there.

18. The Ruthenians, however, who go to the United States of America or to Canada, to exercise spiritual ministry under the jurisdiction of Ordinaries of their own rite, are to observe the special decrees which have been enacted by this Sacred Oriental Congregation.

If for the same ministry they go to the other countries above named, they are to observe the provisions of this Decree.

That this Decree may become fully known to all whom it concerns, it shall become obligatory from the first day of April, 1930.

All the above provisions having been reported to His Holiness in the audience of 22 June and 7 Dec., 1929, His Holiness approved and ratified the same, and ordered this Decree to be issued.

4. Decree—"*Non raro accidit,*" of January 7, 1930[45]

The decree "*Non raro accidit*" of the Sacred Oriental Congregation regarding Oriental clerics, secular or religious, who go from Oriental territories or dioceses to North, Central, or South America, or to Australia, not for the purpose of caring spiritually for the faithful of their own rite, but for some other reason, economic or moral, or simply to stay there for a short time reads as follows:

[45] S.C. pro Eccl. Or.—*AAS,* XXII (1930) 106–108; Bouscaren, *The Canon Law Digest,* I, 24–26.

It not infrequently happens that Oriental clerics, from Oriental territories or dioceses, either with or without permission of this Sacred Oriental Congregation, go to countries in America or Australia, and remain there a long time on every sort of pretext, going from one place to another under pretext of bringing spiritual aid to the faithful of their own race or rite, or of visiting them, sometimes collecting Mass stipends and alms without permission, exercising sacred functions unlawfully, and thus doing no small damage to the reputation of Orientals, especially of Oriental priests. In order, therefore, to protect properly the good name of Oriental priests, and to preclude all occasion of fraud in this regard, this Sacred Congregation, after having discussed the matter in the general session of the Eminent Fathers held on July 17, 1929, has adopted and decreed the following measures:

1. Every priest who is in the above situation shall, through his Superior, or Bishop Ordinary, or Patriarch, send a petition to this Sacred Congregation, and set forth the reason for the petition; he shall indicate also the time that is required for this journey and absence, and the place or places to which he wishes to go; and if there is question of visiting relatives or of transacting temporal business, he shall indicate the domicile of those persons whom he wishes to visit or with whom he wishes to deal.

2. The Superior, Bishop Ordinary, or Patriarch shall, before sending the petition to this Sacred Congregation, add thereto in writing careful notations regarding the life and character of the priest petitioner, giving his judgment as to the truth of the reasons alleged for the petition, and shall provide a *celebret* for the celebration of Mass.

It will be better to send the petition mentioned in Article 1 and the aforesaid notations through the Apostolic Nuntio or Delegate.

3. If this Sacred Congregation—after having received, if need be and it judges the same to be necessary, still further information regarding the priest—shall grant the requested permission, it will send a notice of that fact to the Apostolic Nuntio or Delegate, or, with notice to the latter, will send the formal notice to the Ordinary of the place to which the priest wishes to go and stay; and it will grant the permission to the priest by a rescript given to him personally together with commenda-

tory letters for the celebration of Mass, indicating also the place to which the said priest is about to go, the reasons therefor, and the time of his stay.

4. For urgent cases, in which on account of grave damage or imminent danger there is not time to have recourse to the Sacred Congregation, the same Sacred Congregation grants to the Apostolic Nuntios and Delegates the necessary faculties, according to special instructions given to them.

5. Observing, as regards intermediate points along the way, the provisions made in Article 9 of the Decree of this Sacred Congregation of 23 Dec., 1929,[46] so far as they are applicable, the Ordinary of the place to which the priest goes in order to remain there according to the permission of the Sacred Congregation, can permit him to say Mass according to the notice received from the Sacred Oriental Congregation.

6. But if the Ordinary of the place has not received the notice mentioned in Article 3, then, in order to prevent all fraud, let him not give credit to any letters or documents, even though they purport to proceed from this Sacred Congregation, which the priest or pretended priest may present, nor admit him to the celebration of Mass, and much less to the exercise of the sacred ministry; and, without prejudice to his own rights in the premises, let the Ordinary in such case refer the matter to the Apostolic Nuntio or Delegate of his country or to this Sacred Congregation.

After the lapse of the prescribed time, let the priest return to his own diocese, observing on his return journey the prescriptions of Article 5 above.

7. If, without just cause, the priest remains in the place above mentioned beyond the time prescribed, the Ordinary of the place shall no longer permit him to celebrate Mass, and, without prejudice to his own rights in the premises, shall report the matter to the Apostolic Nuntio or Delegate or to this Sacred Congregation.

8. As regards the collecting or begging of alms, money, or Mass stipends, these priests are absolutely bound by the Decrees of this Sacred Congregation "regarding Oriental clerics who collect or beg alms, money, or Mass stipends outside of Oriental countries and dioceses," given on this 7 Jan. 1930.[47]

---

[46] *AAS,* XXII (1930), 103; Bouscaren, *The Canon Law Digest,* I, 21–22.

[47] The decree next to be reported.

In order that this Decree may become well known to all those whom it concerns, it shall become obligatory from the first day of April, 1930.

All the above provisions having been reported to His Holiness in the audiences of 22 June and 7 Dec., 1929, His Holiness approved and ratified them, and ordered that the Decree be issued.

5. Decree—"*Saepenumero*," of January 7, 1930[48]

The decree "*Saepenumero*" of the Sacred Oriental Congregation regarding Oriental clerics who collect or beg alms, money, or Mass stipends outside of Oriental countries and dioceses, reads as follows:

The Apostolic See has frequently issued regulations and decrees regarding Oriental clerics, and regarding those also who, falsely usurping this title, on one pretext or another leave home and wander through foreign countries, asking alms, begging their way, asking for Mass stipends, sometimes even falsely asserting that they are authorized to keep only part of the stipend and to give back or leave the rest to the offerers themselves, and thus often deceiving both clergy and people. In this matter it is well to repeat and recall to mind the documents which have recently been issued, and especially the Circular Letter issued by the S.C. Prop. Fid. on 1 Jan., 1912,[49] and the *Monitum* recently issued by the Sacred Congregation on 2 April, 1928,[50] besides the provision made by canon 622, § 4, of the Code: namely: "Without an authentic and recent rescript of the Sacred Oriental Congregation, Latin Ordinaries must neither permit any Oriental of any order or dignity whatsoever to collect money in their territory, nor send any subject of theirs for the same purpose into Oriental dioceses."

Nevertheless, since even now very grave frauds of this kind are being devised and perpetrated, especially by those who, being neither clerics nor Orientals, nor Catholics, fraudulently assume those characters; therefore, the regulations which have been already issued are by this present Decree, which has been maturely

[48] S.C. pro Eccl. Or.—*AAS,* XXII (1930), 108–110; Bouscaren, *The Canon Law Digest,* I, 27–28.

[49] *AAS,* IV (1912), 532–533.

[50] This *monitum* is reported in the present Article under no. 1.

considered in the plenary session of the Eminent Fathers of this Sacred Congregation on 17 July, 1929, more fully and explicitly confirmed and explained.

1. In order that any collection, whether of money or of Mass stipends, be made in a Latin diocese by any Oriental cleric of whatsoever order or dignity, the permission of the Sacred Oriental Congregation is absolutely required.

2. The Sacred Oriental Congregation will make it their practice never to grant the permission either to beg money or to collect Mass stipends, for any place or whatever be the reason alleged.

3. If ever, owing to altogether peculiar circumstances and for a quite extraordinary reason, the Sacred Congregation decides to grant such permission, the permission will be limited and restricted to places designated by name; and moreover the Sacred Congregation itself will expressly inform the individual Bishops of places regarding the permission and the reasons therefor; and this without prejudice to the rule that even in this case the collection cannot be made except with the consent of the Bishop.

4. In order, therefore, to avoid all deception in this matter, no Ordinary—unless he shall have been informed in advance by the Holy See as above provided, either directly or through a Legate of the Roman Pontiff, that is a Nuntio or Apostolic Delegate—shall have power to concede or permit in any way that any collection be made within his territory, either of money or of Mass stipends, not even though the person collecting the money have letters of recommendation or any documents whatsoever from other Ordinaries or from any ecclesiastical dignitary, or even though he present documents purporting to be from this Sacred Congregation.

Likewise, neither Ordinaries nor rectors of churches may supply such Orientals or persons claiming to be Orientals with Mass stipends, nor give them the same in any way. And if they do, they are themselves responsible for the celebration of the Masses and also, in proportion to their guilt, for any help they have given these persons in the collection of money or of stipends or intentions of Masses.

5. This decree applies to all Orientals everywhere, excepting those who are in their own Oriental territory.

6. The Most Reverend Ordinaries are requested to inform their priests of this Decree, especially the rectors

of churches, religious houses, and as far as is necessary, also the faithful.

If such cases of abuses occur in their dioceses, they should report the names of those who are passing for Orientals to this Sacred Congregation, and if the matter be urgent and it seem advisable, they should report them also to the civil authorities of the place.

In order that this Decree may become fully known to those whom it may concern, it shall become obligatory from the first day of April, 1930.

All the above provisions having been reported to His Holiness in the audiences of 22 June and 7 Dec., 1929, His Holiness approved and confirmed them, and ordered that the Decree be published.

6. Instruction—"*Quo facilior,*" of September 26, 1932[51]

The Instruction "*Quo facilior*" of the Sacred Oriental Congregation regarding Oriental clerics in foreign countries other than their own Patriarchate or their own country states as follows:

To facilitate the observance of the ancient canons and of the regulations which the Holy See has repeatedly made in regard to Oriental clerics while they are outside their own country, that they may be admitted to celebrate Mass and may win the favor and protection of the Ordinaries of places, the Sacred Oriental Congregation has decided to issue an Instruction containing all together the provisions which are to be observed either by the clerics themselves or by the Ordinaries of places.

Heretofore, by the Decree *Qua sollerti,* of 23 Dec., 1929,[52] rules were enacted for Oriental clerics who go to Australia or to America for the spiritual care of the faithful of their own rite; and by the Decree, *Non raro accidit,* of 7 Jan., 1930,[53] similar regulations were made for clerics who go to those countries for any other reason, economic or moral, and for a short stay.

Without prejudice to or modification of the aforesaid Decrees of this Sacred Congregation, the present letter states briefly the regulations which govern the advent and the stay of any cleric of the Oriental rite,

---

[51] S.C. pro Eccl. Or.—*AAS,* XXIV (1932), 344–346; Bouscaren, *The Canon Law Digest,* I, 39–42.

[52] This decree is reported in the present Article under n. 3.

[53] See n. 2 of the present Article.

whether he be a regular or a secular, in any of the other foreign countries besides his own Patriarchate or his own Oriental country.

1. Every Oriental cleric who wishes to go to foreign countries other than his own Patriarchate or his own country, must, before leaving his diocese, obtain permission or *discessorial letters* from his own Ordinary; and he must also, through his Ordinary, obtain from the Sacred Oriental Congregation *commendatory letters,* which are given by way of rescript, in which shall be mentioned the place to which the said priest is going and the duration of his stay there (can. 804, § 1).

2. Such a priest, while staying in a diocese other than his own, is subject in everything that concerns discipline to the Ordinary of the place, and must obey his orders, without, however, any consequent impairment or diminution of the bond which subjects him to his own Bishop or Patriarch.

3. After the priest in question has come to the diocese mentioned in the rescript of this Sacred Congregation, he may not go from that to another diocese, except for a sufficient reason, which shall be approved both by the Bishop of the diocese where he is, and by the Bishop of the diocese to which he wishes to go; and he must also have the previous consent of both Bishops, and observe exactly all the conditions which they may enjoin.

4. At the expiration of the time stated in the rescript, the priest in question must return to his diocese. "If the priest remains without just cause in the place above mentioned beyond the prescribed time, the Ordinary of the place shall no longer permit him to celebrate Mass, and, without prejudice to his own right in the premises, shall report the matter to the Apostolic Nuntio or Delegate, or to this Sacred Congregation." [54]

5. Such a priest may not exercise the sacred ministry, even incidentally, unless he has been admitted to that diocese for that purpose, or unless at the command or with the express consent of the Ordinary of the place.

6. If the aforesaid priest protract his stay beyond a year in the exercise of the sacred ministry, "at the end of every year, counting from the date of the rescript, he is obliged to send to this Sacred Oriental Congregation a

[54] Decree "*Non raro accidit,*" n. 7, reported under n. 4 of the present Article.

report in writing of the religious state of his people and of his fulfillment of his sacred ministry; he shall show this report to the Ordinary of the place so that the latter may authoritatively approve it in writing, adding his own annotations thereto if he sees fit. The Ordinary himself will then send the report to the Sacred Congregation." [55]

7. The said priest is, as heretofore, forbidden to make any collections, whether by way of alms and money, or by way of Mass stipends, according to the Decree, *Saepenumero,* of 7 Jan., 1930, "regarding Oriental clerics who collect or beg alms, money, or Mass stipends outside of Oriental countries and dioceses." [56]

8. During the priest's journey either to or from the foreign country, the rector of the church where he wishes to celebrate Mass may allow him to do so at his prudent discretion, once or several times, provided the priest in question presents the rescript of the Sacred Oriental Congregation mentioned in n. 1; the said rector is obliged to note on that document the date of the Mass and the name of the church, together with his own signature.

If the said priest stays longer than seems proper, the rector of the church shall give notice of that fact to the Bishop or Ordinary of the place.

The Ordinary of the place shall no longer admit to the celebration of Mass a priest who stays longer than is proper at any intermediate point on his journey, or who gads about from one place to another; and, without prejudice to his own rights in the premises, he shall report the matter to the Apostolic Nuntio or Delegate, or to this Sacred Congregation.

9. The Most Excellent Bishops are earnestly requested to see to the thorough observance of these regulations if they have any priests of the Oriental rite in their dioceses.

The priests themselves must conform at once to these regulations, and if they have no *rescript* from this Sacred Congregation, must secure one; otherwise they can no longer be admitted to celebrate Mass in any diocese outside of their own country.

---

[55] Decree "*Qua sollerti,*" n. 7, reported under n. 3 of the present Article.

[56] Decree "*Saepenumero*" reported under n. 5 of the present Article.

7. Monitum—" Sacrae Congregationi," of July 20, 1937 [57]

The *monitum " Sacrae Congregationi "* contains rules to be observed by clerics of the Oriental rite while they are away from their Patriarchates. It reads as follows:

> It has several times again recently been reported to the Sacred Congregation for the Oriental Church that certain men, fraudulently exhibiting false credentials and using the name and dress of Oriental priests, are wandering about through various lands, begging alms, collecting Mass stipends, and even demanding the right to celebrate the Divine Sacrifice.
>
> Lest these grievous and most sacrilegious impostures produce their deplorable consequences, this same Sacred Congregation most urgently begs Ordinaries of places to remember the regulations and decrees which the Holy See has more than once promulgated to prevent impositions and wrongs of this kind.
>
> They must especially call to mind and observe the following: the Decree, *Qua sollerti,* of 23 Dec., 1929, regarding Oriental clerics who go to countries of America or Australia to minister spiritually to the faithful of their rite; [58] the Decree, *Non raro accidit,* of 7 Jan., 1930, regarding Oriental clerics who go to those same countries for some other reason, economic or moral, and for a short time; [59] the Decree, *Saepenumero,* of 7 Jan., 1930, regarding Oriental clerics who beg alms or collect money or Mass stipends outside Oriental dioceses; [60] the Decree, *Quo facilior,* of 26 Sept., 1932, regarding Oriental clerics outside their own Patriarchates.[61]
>
> These decrees prescribe among other things that no Oriental priest may be admitted to celebrate Mass outside his own Patriarchate unless he presents authentic and unexpired credentials of recommendation from the Sacred Oriental Congregation (see also canon 804, § 1, of the Code of Canon Law), and that no Latin Ordinary may permit in his territory any Oriental cleric, whatever his order and dignity, to collect either money or Mass

[57] S.C. pro Eccl. Or.—*AAS,* XXIX (1937), 342-343; Bouscaren, *The Canon Law Digest,* II, 3-5.

[58] This decree is reported under n. 3 of the present Article.

[59] This decree is reported under n. 4 of the present Article.

[60] This decree is reported under n. 5 of the present Article.

[61] This decree is reported under n. 6 of the present Article.

stipends, without an authentic and recent rescript of the same Sacred Congregation (see also canon 622, § 4, of the Code of Canon Law).

If at any time, because of quite peculiar circumstances, the Sacred Congregation decides to permit the collection of money or Mass stipends, the Congregation itself will notify the Bishops individually and expressly of the fact of such permission and the reason for it. Hence no Ordinary, except in case he should be so notified by the Holy See either directly or through the Legate of the Roman Pontiff, can in any way allow or permit any collections whatever to be made in his territory by Oriental clerics.

If they do so, they themselves will be responsible for the celebration of the Masses, and in proportion to their guilt will be accountable also for the aid supplied as regards the money and the Mass stipends which have been collected. (See the Decree, *Saepenumero,* 7 Jan., 1930; *Acta Apostolicae Sedis,* Vol. 22, p. 109.)

In order the more effectively to prevent all abuses, the Most Excellent Ordinaries are requested to inform their priests, especially rectors of churches, and all religious houses, and as far as necessary also the faithful, regarding these rules.

Given at Rome, from the office of the Sacred Oriental Congregation, July 20, 1937.

APPENDIX I

DECRETUM S. CONGREGATIONIS EPISCOPORUM ET REGULARIUM, DIE 27 MARTII 1896, QUO DEFINIUNTUR NORMAE A SORORIBUS ELEEMOSYNAS QUAERITANTIBUS SERVANDAE[1]

Singulari quidem protectione et auxilio dignae semet exhibent mulieres illae, quae in piis religiosisque Institutis Deo se devovent, ut in proximorum bonum longe lateque opera misericordiae exerceant nedum directe, sed stipem etiam iisdem operibus sustentandis quaeritantes, atque egregiam eapropter humilitatis, patientiae, caritatis aliarumque virtutum laudem praeseferentes. Cum tamen hoc colligendarum eleemosynarum ministerium, prae muliebri quaeritantium indole, ac hodierna humanae societatis conditione, periculis haud vacet nisi opportunis cautelis communiatur, S. Congregatio Episcoporum et Regularium nonnullis Episcopis petentibus, re diligenter et mature perpensa, haec quae sequuntur statuit ac decrevit:

1. In votorum simplicium Institutis opus quaeritandi eleemosynas alumnae non aggrediantur nisi in spiritu fidei, quod stipem non sibi quaerant, sed ipsi Christo Iesu, memores verborum eius: *Quamdiu fecistis uni ex his fratribus meis minimis, mihi fecistis.* Praeterea Ordinarios locorum, etiamsi eorum territoria pertranseant, obsequio, reverentia et devotione prosequantur tanquam parentes et patronos, quod adeant cum fiducia pro consilio, auxilio as praesidio in qualibet necessitate.

2. Iisdem votorum simplicium Sororibus non liceat eleemosynas quaerere sive intra dioecesim in qua ipsae resident, sive extra, sine licentia Ordinarii loci respectivae residentiae.

3. Stipem quaesiturae extra dioecesim respectivae residentiae licentiam obtinere insuper debent ab Ordinario loci in quo eleemosynas quaeritare desiderant.

4. Nihil tamen impedit, quominus Superiorissae, nulla petita

[1] *ASS,* XXVIII (1895-1896), 555-558; *Fontes,* n. 2029.

licentia, ad sublevandam domorum vel piorum operum, quibus praesunt, inopiam, possint eleemosynas undequaque oblatas accepto habere, vel etiam per litteras impetrare ab honestis ac benevolis personis quibuscumque, usquedum a legitimo Superiore, rationabili ex causa, non prohibeantur.

5. Ordinarius loci, in quo exstat domus Sororum quaeritare volentium, licentiam eis non concedat: 1. si de vera domus vel pii operis necessitate sibi non constet; 2. si quaeritatio commode fieri possit per alios ab ipsomet Ordinario designandos. Si autem necessitati occurri valeat per quaeritationem in loco, in quo Sorores resident, vel infra propriam dioecesim, Ordinarius licentiam eisdem non impertiatur eleemosynas colligendi extra dioecesim.

6. Utraque licentia tradatur gratis et in scriptis, in qua quilibet Ordinarius leges et conditiones imponere poterit, quas pro locorum, temporum et personarum adiunctis magis opportunas in Domino iudicaverit. Licentia vero Ordinarii piae Sororum domus contineat litteras vel commissorias ad parochos aliasve prudentes personas, pro Sororibus quaeritantibus intra dioecesim, vel commendatitias ad Ordinarios aliarum dioecesium pro Sororibus extra propriam dioecesim quaeritantibus. In litteris commissoriis mandetur parochis aliisve probis personis, ut consiliis et meliori qua possunt opera praesto sint Sororibus, earum agendi rationem invigilent, et si quid in eis minus rectum resciverint, statim ipsi Ordinario referant. In commendatiis exorentur Ordinarii locorum, ut in sua quisque dioecesi Sorores ad quaeritandum admissas protegat ac adiuvet ac si sibi subditas eas haberet.

7. Quisque loci Ordinarius Sorores ex aliena dioecesi advenientes ad eleemosynas colligendas non admittat, nisi prius eaedem licentiam proprii Ordinarii sibi exhibuerint. Sororibus vero huiusmodi licentiam exhibentibus ipse suam, si lubeat, impertiatur licentiam quaeritandi in propria dioecesi. Ubi autem Sorores, etiamsi utraque licentia praeditae, in eleemosynarum quaestu male se gerant, statim in propriam domum eas redire Ordinarius iubeat, opportunisque etiam mediis, si opus fuerit, compellat.

8. Superiorissae, praesertim extra locum ubi domus habent, numquam ad eleemosynas quaerendas mittant Sorores, nisi binas,

aetate et animo maturas, intra dioecesim non ultra mensem, extra dioecesim non ultra duos menses, et semper ea pecuniae summa instructas qua, inopinato quocumque casu cogente, possint statim domum redire. Sorores quaeritantes semper et ubique ea qua decet, modestia eniteant, virorum familiaritatem et sermones inutiles caveant; clamores, tabernas aliaque loca incongrua evitent; nec in domibus longiorem moram faciant, quam sit necessarium pro exspectandis eleemosynis. Singulae numquam incedant, neque ab invicem separentur, nisi necessitate impellente. Iter facientes, si commode fieri poterit, utantur via ferrea; sed, quantum possunt, de nocte neque ab uno loco discedant, neque ad alium perveniant. De suo adventu futuro praemoneat illum, cui datae sunt Episcopi litterae, eique cum pervenerint se sistant precesque adhibeant, ut intercedat pro invenienda hospitalitate apud aliquod pium feminarum Institutum, vel saltem apud aliquam honestam mulierem, nunquam vero in domo ubi possint in qliquod periculum offendere. Matutinas ac vespertinas preces non omittant: quotidie de mane aliquam ex vicinioribus ecclesiis petant, ibique Sacro assistant: singulis hebdomadis poenitentiae et Eucharistiae sacramentis reficiantur. Ante solis ortum et post occasum eleemosynas per loca non quaeritent. Elapso tempore ad quaeritandum eis praefixo, sine ulla mora ad propriam Superiorissam recto tramite remigrent. Eleemosynas numquam arroganter vel tanquam debitas postulent, sed breviter et humiliter sua et piorum operum exposita inopia, si quid sponte offertur accipiant, secus patienter divinae Providentiae confidant. Alias normas opportunas, quae a propria Superiorissa dari poterunt, adamussim observent.

Datum Romae ex Secretaria memoratae S. Congregationis Episcoporum et Regularium die 27. Martii 1896.

APPENDIX II

DECRETUM S. CONGREGATIONIS RELIGIOSORUM, DIE 21 NOVEMBRIS 1908, QUO IURE ET QUA RATIONE RELIGIOSI SODALES STIPIS QUAERITANDAE MINISTERIUM OBIRE POSSINT ET VALEANT[1]

De eleemosynis colligendis gravis quaestio, quae iam anteactis saeculis non semel agitata fuit, hodie praesertim, ob peculiaria rerum ac temporum adiuncta, in praxi maiores ac frequentiores praesefert difficultates. Quibus ut occurreret, S. Congregatio Episcoporum et Regularium, omnibus mature perpensis, die 27 martii 1896 promulgavit decretum *Singulari quidem,* quo colligendarum eleemosynarum ministerium opportunis pro hodierna humanae societatis conditione communiebatur cautelis. Attamen mulierum dumtaxat respiciebat Sodalitates. Quo autem et virorum Institutis religiosis melius provideretur, eidem Sacrae Congregationi, in plenario consessu die 8 maii anni 1908 habito, visum est pro his quoque nonnullas apponere quaestuationum normas, quas, ex Secretaria supradictae Congregationis Episcoporum et Regularium acceptas, sacra Congregatio Negotiis Religiosorum Sodalium praeposita, de mandato Smi Domini Nostri Pii divina Providentia Pp. X, publici iuris facit.

I. Quod Ordines Mendicantes

1. Regulares, qui Mendicantes vocantur et sunt, ex institutione Sedis Apostolicae cum sola licentia Superiorum suorum eleemosynas quaerere valeant in dioecesi, ubi erectus est conventus. Ordinariorum licentia necessario censenda est data in ipso actu quo conventus fundationi consensum praebuerunt.

2. Si vero iidem Regulares extra dioecesim, ubi conventus habent, stipem quaeritare velint, Ordinarii illius dioeceseos licentia, per suos Superiores in scriptis obtenta, indigent.

[1] *AAS,* I (1909), 153–156; *Fontes,* n. 4391.

3. Ordinarii praecipue limitrophes, hanc licentiam absque gravioribus urgentioribusque causis ne denegent, si aliquis conventus ex quaestuatione in sola dioecesi, ubi erectus est, vivere nullimodo possit, ut in parvis dioecesibus contingere solet.

4. Quae licentia intelligitur habitualis, usque nempe ad expressam revocationem; quae quidem revocatio, ut par est, nonnisi legitimis de causis, iisque tantum perdurantibus, facienda est.

5. Ut Mendicantes praefato iure gaudeant, per seipsos, non autem per personas Ordini extraneas, eleemosynas colligere debent.

6. Regulares quaestuantes semper secum habere debent litteras authenticas, quibus constet de debita facultate deque officio quaestuationis sibi commisso. Quas litteras parochis ultro exhibere tenentur; necnon Ordinariis, quoties ab ipsis requirantur.

7. Non licet Superioribus regularibus ad hoc opus mittere nisi Religiosos aetate et animo maturos; numquam eos qui studiis adhunc incumbunt.

8. Religiosi eleemosynas collecturi ne pergant soli sed bini, praesertim extra urbem seu locum ubi habent conventum, seclusa gravis necessitatis causa; quo in casu quaestuarius publice notus sit oportet atque aetate, virtute ac fidelium existimatione omnino commendatus.

9. Porro extra locum conventuum quaestuantes, apud parochos vel apud alios clericos saeculares vel regulares, aut, iis deficientibus, apud aliquem pium benefactorem, christiana honestate et virtute conspicuum, divertant.

10. Extra propriam domum ne maneant ultra mensem, si in propria dioecesi; non ultra duos, si in alia eleemosynas quaerant; neque iidem denuo mittantur, nisi postquam per unum, vel respective per duos menses, vitam communem iuxta regulam et constitutiones in conventu exegerint, prout uno vel duobus mensibus extra claustra degere debuerunt.

11. Qui in ipso loco, ubi situs est conventus, stipem corrogant, noctu extra propriam domum nequaquam manebunt.

12. Religiosi quaestuantes semper illa, qua decet, humilitate, modestia, munditie eniteant; saecularium, praesertim mulierum cuiuscumque sint conditionis, familiaritatem caveant; loca suae professioni minime congrua omnino devitent; pietatem sincere

foveant atque spiritualia exercitia in religione ipsorum solita pro viribus fideliter adimpleant.

13. Superiores regulares, graviter onerata eorum conscientia, ne omittant quaestuariis suis normas agendi, quas prudentia suadet, opportunas praescribere.

14. Si vero, quod absit, Regulares quaestuantes notorie deliquerint, fidelibus scandalum praebuerint, vel etiam contra legitimam prohibitionem eleemosynas colligere ausi fuerint, Ordinarius loci iubeat eos in propriam domum redire atque etiam tanquam Sedis Apostolicae Delegatus Superiores moneat, ut illos corrigant et pro gravitate scandali puniant; quod si secus fecerint, quam primum ad Sanctam Sedam recurrat.

II. Quoad Ordines vel Instituta Religiosa non-Mendicantium

1. Religiosi sive Ordinum sive congregationum *iuris pontificii,* qui privilegium quaeritandi eleemosynas neque vi propriarum Constitutionum a Sancta Sede approbatarum, neque vi Apostolicae concessionis gaudent, veniam Apostolicae Sedis impetrare debent, ut quaestuationes instituere valeant; praeterea licentiam per suos Superiores ab Ordinario loci obtinere tenentur, nisi forte Sancta Sedes in hoc expresse et specialiter iuri Episcopi derogaverit, quod numquam praesumi potest, sed indubitatis documentis probari debet.

2. Religiosi vero qui sunt *iuris dioecesani,* opus colligendi eleemosynas nequaquam aggredi poterunt, nisi licentiam obtinuerint tum ab Ordinario loci in quo resident, tum etiam, si extra dioecesim propriae residentiae abituri sint, ab Ordinario loci in quo stipem quaerere desiderant.

3. Ordinarii autem locorum, si opportunum visum fuerit pro unaquaque domo cuiusque religiosi suae dioeceseos Instituti, sive iuris pontificii sive iuris dioecesani, e mendicato viventis, limites quaestuationis constituere possunt et respective servandos curare, praesertim ubi sunt conventus Regularium nomine et re Mendicantium; nec huiusmodi Religiosis non-Mendicantibus quaeritandi licentiam concedant, nisi sibi constet de vera domus vel pii operis necessitate, cui alio modo occurri nequeat; et si necessitatibus provideri potest per quaestuationem in loco vel districtu, in

quo Religiosi resident, aut intra dioecesim, instituendam, ampliorem licentiam nequaquam concedant.

4. Ordinarius porro illius dioeceseos, ad quam isti Religiosi aliarum dioeceseon eleemosynas quaesituri accedant, collectas eis minime permittat, nisi prius per se vel per suos ad hoc delegatos, praeter litteras obedientiales proprii Superioris, facultatem, vel Apostolicae Sedis si sunt iuris pontificii, vel proprii Ordinarii si sunt iuris dioecesani, recognoverit et huius decreti praescriptis conformen invenerit.

5. Insuper Ordinarius sedulo advertat, utrum Religiosi qui pro Missionibus exteris subsidia quaerunt, praeter litteras commendatitias Vicarii vel Praefecti Apostolici respectivae Missionis et litteras obedientiales Moderatoris generalis proprii Instituti, habeant quoque facultatem a S. Congregatione de Propaganda Fide in forma authentica recenter datam.

6. Licentiam colligendi eleemosynas Ordinarii concedant gratis et in scriptis; notatis semper (sive ad calcem litterarum obedientalium sive in documento separato) tum nominibus Religiosorum, qui ad colligendas eleemosynas designati sunt, tum nomine Ordinis vel Instituti ad quod pertinent, tum loco et tempore pro quibus licentia vaiitura sit.

7. Licentias loco et tempore generales Religiosis huiusmodi nequequam concedant Ordinarii, sed potius invigilabunt, ne sive quaestuantes, sive praetextu quaestuationis, extra propriam domum maneant ultra mensem, si in propria dioecesi; aut ultra duos menses, si in aliena eleemosynas quaerant; neve iidem denuo mittantur, nisi postquam per unum, respective duos menses, in suo conventu degerint, prout uno vel duobus mensibus foris manserant.

8. Ut Religiosi Ordinariorum facultate colligendi eleemosynas uti valeant, id per se, non per alios, facere debent.

9. Ad haec et ipsi fideliter observent, quae supra pro Religiosis Ordinum Mendicantium sancita sunt, parte I, art. 6, 7, 8, 9, 11, 12, 13.

10. In casu tandem, quo hi Religiosi quaestuantes contra legitimam prohibitionem eleemosynas collegerint, vel, quod Deus avertat, male se gesserint scandalove fidelibus fuerint, Ordinarius loci, etiam tanquam Sedis Apostolicae Delegatus, eos pro gravitate

delicti et scandali opportunis remediis coërceat et in propriam domum a suis Superioribus puniendos remittat.

Datum Romae, ex Secretaria supradictae Sacrae Congregationis Negotiis Religiosorum Sodalium praepositae, in festo Praesentationis B.M.V., die 21 Novembris 1908.

CONCLUSIONS

1. The justification of alms-gathering by religious depends upon necessity. This necessity may arise (a) *per modum status,* as is the case with such religious whose institutes do not possess any title or right to subsistence except the uncertain income derived from mendicancy; (b) *per modum actus,* as is the case with religious institutes which, though they are entitled to possess movable and immovable property, do not derive from such titles a sufficient income for their own subsistence and for the support of the pious and charitable works entrusted to their care.

2. Mendicants, who are such in name and in fact, may solicit alms with the sole permission of their superior within the diocese in which their house is situated. However, the words *religiosa domus* in canon 621 must be taken in their most obvious sense, as meaning only a canonically erected house. In the erection of other houses which do not require canonical erection the permission to solicit alms cannot be presumed as it can when the local Ordinary gives permission for the erection of a house in the canonical sense of canon 497, § 1.

3. The expression *licentia Superiorum suorum* in canon 621 includes the local superior of a *domus* in the formal technical sense of canon 497, § 1, and higher superiors. The power of the superior who enjoys the right to grant permission to solicit alms without the consent of the local Ordinary extends only to the diocese in which the canonically erected house is situated and to which the religious themselves belong either through profession or residence.

4. Nuns with simple vows and not subject to the papal enclosure are obliged to observe the special instructions of the Sacred Congregation of Bishops and Regulars given in the decree *"Singulari quidem,"* even though this decree mentions only sisters (*sorores*) of institutes with simple vows.

5. In alms-gathering mendicants who are such in name and in fact, as well as other religious who enjoy a similar privilege by

their Constitutions or by apostolic Indult, can in no manner be restricted by local Ordinaries either individually, as in diocesan laws, or collectively, as in provincial or plenary Councils as long as they collect alms in the diocese in which the religious house is canonically erected.

6. The collecting of alms by methods not comprehended under the juridic concept of alms-gathering is governed by canon 1503 even as to mendicants in the strict sense. Canon 1503 forbids private individuals, both clerics and laymen, to collect alms for any charitable or ecclesiastical purpose without the written permission of the Holy See or of their own proper Ordinary and of the Ordinary of the place where the collection is to be made.

7. By Orientals in canon 622, § 4, are meant not merely religious but all Catholics who belong to an Oriental rite regardless of where they may have their residence or affiliation to a certain rite.

8. The decree of the III Plenary Council of Baltimore in forbidding priests, secular and religious, who come from abroad without proper authorization to collect alms, to say Mass, not even once, without the permission of the local Ordinary is not contrary to the Code of Canon Law and is still effective. This decree of the Council is also binding on Oriental priests.

BIBLIOGRAPHY

Sources

Acta Apostolicae Sedis, Commentarium Officiale, Romae 1909–.

Acta et Decreta Concilii Plenarii Baltimorensis III (1894). Baltimorae, 1886.

Acta Sanctae Sedis, 41 vols., Romae, 1865–1908.

Bouscaren, T. Lincoln, *The Canon Law Digest,* 2 vols., Milwaukee: The Bruce Publishing Co., 1934–1943.

Bullarium Franciscanum, 8 vols., Romae, 1759–1908.

Bullarium Ordinis Praedicatorum sub auspiciis SS. D.N.D. Benedicti XIII, 8 vols., Romae, 1729–1740.

Bullarium Pontificium S. Congregationis de Propaganda Fide, 5 vols, Romae, 1839–1841.

Bullarum Diplomatum et Privilegiorum Sanctorum Romanorum Pontificum Taurinensis Editio, 24 vols. et Appendix Augustae Taurinorum, 1857–1872.

Canones et Decreta Sacrosancti Oecumenici Concilii Tridentini, Romae, 1904.

Codex Iuris Canonici, Pii X Pontificis Maximi iussu digestus Benedicti Papae XV auctoritate promulgatus, ed. Petri Card. Gasparri, Romae: Typis Polyglottis Vaticanis, 1917: Reimpressio, 1930.

Codicis Iuris Canonici Fontes cura Emi Petri Card. Gasparri editi, 9 vols., Romae (later Civitate Vaticana): Typis Polyglottis, 1923–1939. Vols. VII–IX *ed. cura et studio Emi Iustiniani Card. Serédi.*

Collectanea in usum Secretariae Sacrae Congregationis Episcoporum et Regularium, cura A. Bizzarri, Romae, 1885.

Collectanea S. Congregationis de Propaganda Fide, 2 vols., Romae, 1907.

Constitutiones Ordinis Fratrum Minorum Sancti Patris Francisci Conventualium, Romae: Ad SS. XII Apostolos, 1932.

Decretales Gregorii Papae IX, una cum Glossis Restitutae, Romae, 1582.

Jaffé, Philippus, *Regesta Pontificum Romanorum ab condita Ecclesia ad annum post Christum natum MCXCVIII, ed. 2, correctam et auctam auspiciis Gulielmi Wattenbach curaverunt S. Loewenfeld, F. Kaltenbrunner, P. Ewald,* 2 vols. in 1, Lipsiae, 1885–1888.

Liber Sextus Decretalium una cum Clementinis et Extravagantibus Earumque Glossis Restitutis, Romae, 1582.

Mansi, Ioannes, *Sacrorum Conciliorum Nova et Amplissima Collectio,* 53 vols. in 60, Paris, Arnhem, Leipzig, 1901–1927.

Normae secumdum quas Sacra Congregatio in novis religiosis Congregationibus approbandis procedere solet—AAS, XIII (1921), 312–319.

Potthast, Augustus, *Regesta Pontificum Romanorum, inde ab A. post Christum natum MCXCVIII ad A. MCCCIV*, 2 vols., Berolini, 1874–1875.

Regula Primitiva et Constitutiones Fratrum Discalceatorum Ordinis Sanctissimae Trinitatis Redemptionis Captivorum, Isola del Liri: Soc. Tip. a Maioce & Pisani, 1933.

Regulae et Constitutiones Fratrum Discalceatorum Ordinis Beatissimae Virginis de Monte Carmelo, Romae: Typis Polyglottis Vaticanis, 1928.

The Rule and General Constitutions of the Friars Minor, Paterson, New Jersey: St. Anthony Guild Press, 1936.

Reference Works

Acta Capitulorum Generalium Ordinis Praedicatorum recensuit B. M. Reichert in *Monumenta Ordinis Praedicatorum Historia*, Tomus III, Romae, 1898–1899.

Amiaud, Arthur, *La Légende Syriaque de S. Alexis, L'Homme de Dieu*, Paris, 1899.

Augustine, Charles, *A Commentary on the New Code of Canon Law*, 8 vols., Vol. III, 2. ed., St. Louis: Herder Book Co., 1919.

———, *The Pastor according to the New Code of Canon Law*, St. Louis: Herder Book Co., 1924.

Ayrinhac, H. A., *Administrative Legislation in the New Code of Canon Law*, London, New York, Toronto: Longmans Green and Co., 1930.

Balme-Lelaidier, *Cartulaire ou histoire diplomatique de St. Dominique*, 2 vols., Paris, 1892.

Balthasar, Karl, *Geschichte des Armutsstreites im Franziskanerorden bis zum Konzil von Vienne*, Muenster, 1911.

Barbosa, Augustinus, *Collectanea Doctorum in Concilium Tridentinum*, Lugduni, 1672.

———, *Iuris Ecclesiastici Universi Libri Tres*, Lugduni, 1672.

Benedictus XIV, *De Synodo Diocesana*, 2. ed., 4 vols., Mechliniae, 1842.

Beste, Udalricus, *Introductio in Codicem*, editio altera, Collegeville, Minn: St. John's Abbey Press, 1944.

Blat, Albertus, *Commentarium Textus Codicis Iuris Canonici*, 5 vols. in 6, Romae, 1921–1927.

Bonaventura, St., *Opera Omnia*, 8 vols., Ad Claras Aquas, 1882–1898.

Borkowski, Aurelius, *De Confraternitatibus Ecclesiasticis*, The Catholic University of America Canon Law Studies, n. 3, Washington, D. C.: The Catholic University of America, 1918.

Catholic Encyclopedia, The, 16 vols. and 3 suppls., New York, 1907–1922.

Chelodi, Ioannes, *Ius De Personis iuxta Codicem Iuris Canonici*, ed. altera a Sac. Ernesto Bertagnolli recognita et aucta, Tridentini: Libr. Edit. Tridentum, 1927.

Cicognani, Hamletus J., *Commentarium ad Librum I Codicis*, Romae: Ex Schola Typographica "Pio X," 1925.

Clancy, Patrick, *The Local Religious Superior,* The Catholic University of America Canon Law Studies, n. 175, Washington, D. C.: The Catholic University of America Press, 1943.

Corornata, Matthaeus, Conte a, *Compendium Iuris Canonici,* 2 vols., Taurini: Marietti, 1937-1938.

——, *Institutiones Iuris Canonici,* 5 vols., Taurini: Marietti, 1928-1936; Vols. I-II, 2. ed., 1939.

Creusen, Joseph—Garesché, Edward F.—Ellis, Adam C., *Religious Men and Women in the Code,* 3. ed., Milwaukee: Bruce, 1940.

Cuthbert, Fr., O.S.F.C., *St. Francis and Poverty,* New York, 1910.

Dausend Hugo, *Das interrituelle Recht im Codex Iuris Canonici,* Görres-Gesellschaft Veröffentlichungen der Sektion für Rechts—und Staatswissenschaft, 79. Heft, Paderborn: Schöningh, 1939.

Davison, E. Scott, *Some Forerunners of St. Francis Assisi,* Boston and New York: Houghton Mifflin Co., 1927.

Delatte, Paul, *Commentary on the Rule of St. Benedict,* London: Burns Oates & Washborne Limited, 1921.

De Vita Regulari, edita curante Joachim Berthier, O.P., Romae, 1888-1889.

Doheny, William J., *Church Property: Modes of Acquisition,* The Catholic University of America Canon Law Studies, n. 41, Washington, D. C.: The Catholic University of America, 1927.

Döllinger, Johann, *Sektengeschichte,* 2 vols., München, 1890.

Dubois, Leo, *Saint Francis of Assisi, Social Reformer,* New York, Cincinnati, Chicago: Benziger Brothers, 1906.

Duskie, John A., *The Canonical Status of the Orientals in the United States,* The Catholic University of America Canon Law Studies, n. 48, Washington, D. C.: The Catholic University of America, 1928.

Fagnanus, Prosper, *Ius Canonicum seu Commentaria Absolutissima in Decretalium Libros,* 3 vols. Venetiis, 1709.

Fanfani, Ludovicus, *Le Iure Religiosorum ad Normam Codicis Iuris Canonici,* 2. ed., Taurini-Romae: Marietti, 1925.

Felder, H., *The Ideals of St. Francis of Assisi,* translated by Bermans Bittle, New York, Cincinnati, Chicago: Benziger Brothers, 1925.

Ferraris, Lucius, *Prompta Bibliotheca Canonica, Iuridica, Moralis, Theologica, necnon Ascetica, Polemica, Rubricistica, Historica,* 11 vols., Venetiis, 1782-1794.

Gauchat, Patrick, *Cardinal Bertrand de Turre: His Participation in the Theoretical Controversy concerning the Poverty of Christ and the Apostles under Pope John XXII,* Tipografia Poliglotta Vaticana, 1930.

Giraldus, Ubaldus, *Expositio Iuris Pontificii,* 2 vols., Romae, 1829.

Gonzales-Tellez, Emmanuel, *Commentaria in quinque Libros Decretalium,* 5 vols., Lugduni, 1749.

Hefele, Karl, *Conciliengeschichte,* 2. ed., 9 vols., Freiburg im Breisgau, 1873-1890.

Heimbucher, Max, *Die Orden und Kongregationen der katholischen Kirche,* 3. ed., 2 vols., Paderborn: Ferdinand Schöningh, 1933–1934.

Holzapfel, Heribert, *Manuale Historiae Ordinis Fratrum Minorum,* Freiburg, 1909.

Hostiensis (Henricus de Segusio), *Commentaria in quinque libros Decretalium,* 5 vols. in 3, Venetiis, 1581.

Humbertus de Romanis, *De Vita Regulari,* edita curante Joachim Berthier, 2 vols., Romae, 1888–1889.

Hugo, ———, *Vie de St. Norbert,* Luxembourg, 1704.

Kazenberger, Killian, *The Book of Life,* 3. ed., Paterson, N. J., 1905.

Kirchenlexikon, Wetzer and Welte's, 12 vols., Freiburg im Breisgau, 1882–1901.

Kowalski, Romuald, *Sustenance of Religious Houses of Regulars,* The Catholic University of America Canon Law Studies, n. 199, Washington, D. C.: The Catholic University of America Press, 1944.

Lambermond, H. C., *Der Armutsgedanke des hl. Dominikus und seines Ordens,* Zwolle, Holland: Verlag Waanders, 1926.

Mabillon, Jean, *Annales Ordinis S. Benedicti,* ed. Lucca, 6 vols., Lucca, 1739–1745.

Mann, Horace, *The Lives of the Popes in the Middle Ages,* 18 vols., St. Louis: Herder Book Co., 1902–1932.

Masetti, Pius, *Monumenta et Antiquitates Veteris Disciplinae Ordinis Praedicatorum ab Anno 1216 ad 1348,* 2 vols., Romae, 1864.

Michaud, François, *The History of the Crusades,* translated from the French by Robson, 3 vols., New York, 1853.

McManus, James, *The Administration of Temporal Goods in Religious Institutes,* The Catholic University of America Canon Law Studies, n. 109, Washington, D. C.: The Catholic University of America, 1931,

Migne, P. J., *Patrologiae Cursus Completus, Series Latina,* 221 vols., Parisiis, 1844–1864.

———, *Patrologiae Cursus Completus, Series Graeca,* 161 vols., Parisiis, 1857–1866.

Monacelli, Fr., *Formularium Legale Practicum,* 4 vols., Venetiis, 1736.

Moneta Cremonensis, *Adversus Catharos et Waldenses,* Romae, 1753.

Mostazo, (A) Franciscus, *De Causis Piis,* Lugduni, 1686.

Müller, Karl, *Die Waldenser und ihre einzelnen Gruppen bis zum Anfang des 14ten Jahrhunderts,* Gotha, 1886.

O'Brien, Joseph, *The Exemption of Religious in Church Law,* Milwaukee: The Bruce Publishing Company, 1942.

Opuscula Sancti Patris Francisci Assisiensis, a PP. Collegii S. Bonaventurae, Ad Claras Aquas, 1904.

Ott, A., *Thomas von Aquin und das Mendikantentum,* Freiburg im Breisgau, 1908.

Pennacchi, Joseph, *Commentaria in Constitutionem "Apostolicae Sedis,"* 2 vols., Romae, 1910.

Piatus Montensis (Jean Joseph Laiseaux), *Praelectiones Iuris Regularis,* 2 vols., Tornaci, 1890.

Pierron, J. B., *Die katholischen Armen,* Freiburg im Breisgau, 1911.

Pignatelli, Jacobus, *Consultationes Canonicae,* 4 vols., Venetiis, 1716–1722.

Quetif-Echard, *Scriptores Ordinis Praedicatorum,* Paris, 1719.

Sabatier, Paul, *Life of St. Francis,* New York, 1894.

Schaaf, Valentine, *The Cloister,* The Catholic University of America Canon Law Studies, n. 13, Washington, D. C.: The Catholic University of America, 1921.

Schaefer, P. Timotheus, *De Religiosis ad Normam Codicis Iuris Canonici,* 3. ed., Romae: S.A.L.E.R., 1940.

Scheuermann, Audomar, *Die Exemption nach geltendem Kirchlichen Recht,* Görres-Gesellschaft Veröffentlichungen der Sektion für Rechts— und Staatswissenschaft, 77. Heft, Paderborn: Schöningh, 1938.

Schlee, Ernst, *Die Päpste und die Kreuzzüge,* Halle, 1893.

Schnürer, Gustav, *Kirche und Kultur im Mittelalter,* 2 vols., Paderborn: Ferdinand Schöningh, 1929.

Soldati, Fr., *SS. Thomae et Bonaventurae opuscula adversus Gulielmum de S. Amore,* Romae, 1733.

Suarez, Franciscus, *Opera Omnia,* ed. nova, 28 vols., Parisiis, 1856–1861.

Thomas Aquinas, St., *Sancti Thomae Aquinatis Doctoris Angelici Opera Omnia Iussu Impensaque Leonis XIII, P.M. Edita,* Romae: 1882–; *Contra Gentiles,* Romae, 1882; *Summa Theologica,* Romae, 1888–1906.

Thomas de Celano, *S. Francisci Assisiensis vita et miracula,* edita curante Eduardo Alenconiensis, Romae, 1896.

Turner, Sidney, *The Vow of Poverty,* The Catholic University of America Canon Law Studies, n. 54, Washington, D. C.: The Catholic University of America, 1929.

Vermeersch, A.-Creusen, J., *Epitome Iuris Canonici cum Commentariis ad Scholas et ad Usum Privatum,* 3 vols., 5. ed., Mechlinae-Romae: Dessain, 1933–1936.

Wernz, F.-Vidal, Petrus, *Ius Canonicum ad Codicis Normam Exactum,* 7 vols. in 8, Romae: apud Aedes Universitatis Gregorianae, 1923–1938.

Woywod, Stanislaus, *A Practical Commentary on the Code of Canon Law,* 2 vols., 2. ed., New York: Joseph F. Wagner, Inc., 1926.

Articles

Bäumker, Cl., "Wilhelm von St. Amour,"—*Kirchenlexikon,* XII, 1580–1586.

Denifle, Heinrich, "Die Konstitutionem des Predigerordens vom Jahre 1228,"—*ALKG,* I (1885), 165–193.

Fryar, John, "The Religious Military Orders,"—*ER,* XLVI (1912), 673–683.

Goyeneche, S., ——— in *CpR,* XI (1930), 81–82.

Hefele, K., "Almosenprediger,"—*Kirchenlexikon,* I, 576.

Heiner, F., "Das Kollektieren seitens der Ordensleute,"—*AKKR,* XCI (1911), 95–110.

Jorder, J. Chr., "Das Sammeln von Almosen durch Ordensfrauen,"—*AKKR,* LXXVI (1896), 105–109.

Kirsch, J. P., "Alexius, Saint and Confessor,"—*Catholic Encyclopedia, The,* I, 307–308.

Larraona, A., ———, in *CpR,* IV (1923), 12; in *CpR,* XII (1931), 253.

Mannucci, Ubaldus, "Commentarium Statuorum de Quaestuatione,"—*Analecta Ecclesiastica,* XVII (1909), 4–10.

———, "De Iure et Ratione Quaestuandi,"—*Analecta Ecclesiastica,* XVII (1909), 72–80.

———, "De Historia Iuris Quaestuandi," *Analecta Ecclesiastica,* XVII (1909), 288–292.

———, "Members of Religious Orders Collecting Funds,"—*ER,* XL (1908), 414.

Periodicals

Analecta Ecclesiastica, Romae, 1893–1911.

Analecta Sacri Ordinis Fratrum Praedicatorum seu Vetera Ordinis Monumenta Recentioraque Acta, Romae, 1893–; ab anno 1907: *Analecta Sacri Ordinis Fratrum Praedicatorum.*

Archiv für katholisches Kirchenrecht, Innsbruck, 1857–1861; Mainz, 1862–.

Archiv für Literatur und Kirchengeschichte, Berlin, 1885–1890.

Commentarium pro Religiosis, Romae, 1920–; ab anno 1935: *Commentarium pro Religiosis et Missionariis.*

Periodica de Re Canonica et Morali utili praesertim Religiosis et Missionariis, Bruges, 1905–; ab anno 1927: *Periodica de Re Canonica, Morali, Liturgica.*

Theologische Quartalschrift, Linz, 1832–.

ABBREVIATIONS

AAS—*Acta Apostolicae Sedis.*
AKKR—*Archiv für katholisches Kirchenrecht.*
ASS—*Acta Sanctae Sedis.*
BRT—*Bullarum Diplomatum et Privilegiorum Romanorum Pontificum Taurinensis Editio.*
CpR—*Commentarium pro Religiosis.*
CpRM—*Commentarium pro Religiosis et Missionariis.*
ER—*Ecclesiastical Review.*
Fontes—*Codicis Iuris Canonici Fontes cura . . . Gaspari editi.*
MPG—Migne, *Patrologia, Series Graeca.*
MPL—Migne, *Patrologia, Series Latina.*
P.C.I.—Pontificia Commissio ad Codicis Canones authentice interpretandos.
S.C.C.—Sacra Congregatio Concilii.
S.C. de Prop. Fide—Sacra Congregatio de Propaganda Fide.
S.C. Ep. et Reg.—Sacra Congregatio Episcoporum et Regularium.
S.C. pro Eccl. Or.—Sacra Congregatio pro Ecclesia Orientali.
S.C. Rel.—Sacra Congregatio de Religiosis.

INDEX

BIOGRAPHICAL NOTE

Louis G. Meyer was born on September 12, 1906, at Dedham, Iowa. After completing his elementary education at St. Joseph's school, Dedham, Iowa, he attended Conception Seminary, Conception, Missouri, where he received the A.B. degree in June, 1929. In August, 1926, he entered the Benedictine Order at Conception, Missouri. His theological studies were pursued at St. John's University, Collegeville, Minnesota, where he received the S.T.B. degree in June, 1933. He was ordained to the priesthood at Conception, Missouri, on June 5, 1932. After five years of teaching and parochial work he entered the School of Canon Law at the Catholic University of America, and received the Baccalaureate in June, 1939, and the Licentiate in June, 1940.

CANON LAW STUDIES

1. Freriks, Rev. Celestine A. C.PP.S., J.C.D., Religious Congregations in Their External Relations, 121 pp., 1916.
2. Galliher, Rev. Daniel M., O.P., J.C.D., Canonical Elections, 117 pp., 1917.
3. Borkowski, Rev. Aurelius L., O.F.M., J.C.D., De Confraternitatibus Ecclesiasticis, 136 pp., 1918.
4. Castillo, Rev. Cayo, J.C.D., Disertacion Historico-Canonica sobre la Potestad del Cabildo en Sede Vacante o Impedida del Vicario Capitular, 99 pp., 1919 (1918).
5. Kubelbeck, Rev. William J., S.T.B., J.C.D., The Sacred Penitentiaria and Its Relation to Faculties of Ordinaries and Priests, 129 pp., 1918.
6. Petrovits, Rev. Joseph, J. C., S.T.D., J.C.D., The New Church Law on Matrimony, X-461 pp., 1919.
7. Hickey, Rev. John J., S.T.B., J.C.D., Irregularities and Simple Impediments in the New Code of Canon Law, 100 pp., 1920.
8. Klekotka, Rev. Peter J., S.T.B., J.C.D., Diocesan Consultors, 179 pp., 1920.
9. Wanenmacher, Rev. Francis, J.C.D., The Evidence in Ecclesiastical Procedure Affecting the Marriage Bond, 1920 (Printed 1935).
10. Golden, Rev. Henry Francis, J.C.D., Parochial Benefices in the New Code, IV-119 pp., 1921 (Printed 1925).
11. Koudelka, Rev. Charles J., J.C.D., Pastors, Their Rights and Duties According to the New Code of Canon Law, 211 pp., 1921.
12. Melo, Rev. Antonius, O.F.M., J.C.D., De Exemptione Regularium, X-188 pp., 1921.
13. Schaaf, Rev. Valentine Theodore, O.F.M., S.T.B., J.C.D., The Cloister, X-180 pp., 1921.
14. Burke, Rev. Thomas Joseph, S.T.D., J.C.D., Competence in Ecclesiastical Tribunals, IV-117 pp., 1922.
15. Leech, Rev. George Leo, J.C.D., A Comparative Study of the Constitution "Apostolicae Sedis" and the "Codex Juris Canonici," 179 pp., 1922.
16. Motry, Rev. Hubert Louis, S.T.D., J.C.D., Diocesan Faculties According to the Code of Canon Law, II-167 pp., 1922.
17. Murphy, Rev. George Lawrence, J.C.D., Delinquencies and Penalties in the Administration and the Reception of the Sacraments, IV-121 pp., 1923.

* Below n. 100 only the following numbers are still available: Nos. 25, 57 and 75. Beginning with n. 100 only the following numbers are unavailable: Nos. 100–111 inclusive, 113 and 115–117 inclusive.

18. O'Reilly, Rev. John Anthony, S.T.B., J.C.D., Ecclesiastical Sepulture in the New Code of Canon Law, II-129 pp., 1923.
19. Michalicka, Rev. Wenceslas Cyril, O.S.B., J.C.D., Judicial Procedure in Dismissal of Clerical Exempt Religious, 107 pp., 1923.
20. Dargin, Rev. Edward Vincent, S.T.B., J.C.D., Reserved Cases According to the Code of Canon Law, IV-103 pp., 1924.
21. Godfrey, Rev. John A., S.T.B., J.C.D., The Right of Patronage According to the Code of Canon Law, 153 pp., 1924.
22. Hagedorn, Rev. Francis Edward, J.C.D., General Legislation on Indulgences, II-154 pp., 1924.
23. King, Rev. James Ignatius, J.C.D., The Administration of the Sacraments to Dying Non-Catholics, V-141 pp., 1924.
24. Winslow, Rev. Francis Joseph, O.F.M., J.C.D., Vicars and Prefects Apostolic, IV-149 pp., 1924.
25. Correa, Rev. Jose Servelion, S.T.L., J.C.D., La Potestad Legislativa de la Iglesia Catolica, IV-127 pp., 1925.
26. Dugan, Rev. Henry Francis, A.M., J.C.D., The Judiciary Department of the Diocesan Curia, 87 pp., 1925.
27. Keller, Rev. Charles Frederick, S.T.B., J.C.D., Mass Stipends, 167 pp., 1925.
28. Paschang, Rev. John Linus, J.C.D., The Sacramentals According to the Code of Canon Law, 129 pp., 1925.
29. Piontek, Rev. Cyrillus, O.F.M., S.T.B., J.C.D., De Indulto Exclaustrationis necnon Saecularizationis, XIII-289 pp., 1925.
30. Kearney, Rev. Richard Joseph, S.T.B., J.C.D., Sponsors at Baptism According to the Code of Canon Law, IV-127 pp., 1925.
31. Bartlett, Rev. Chester Joseph, A.M., LL.B., J.C.D., The Tenure of Parochial Property in the United States of America, V-108 pp., 1926.
32. Kilker, Rev. Adrian Jerome, J.C.D., Extreme Unction, V-425 pp., 1926.
33. McCormick, Rev. Robert Emmett, J.C.D., Confessors of Religious, VIII-266 pp., 1926.
34. Miller, Rev. Newton Thomas, J.C.D., Founded Masses According to the Code of Canon Law, VII-93 pp., 1926.
35. Roelker, Rev. Edward G., S.T.D., J.C.D., Principles of Privilege According to the Code of Canon Law, XI-166 pp., 1926.
36. Bakalarczyk, Rev. Richardus, M.I.C., J.U.D., De Novitiatu, VIII-208 pp., 1927.
37. Pizzuti, Rev. Lawrence, O.F.M., J.U.L., De Parochis Religiosis, 1927. (Not Printed.)
38. Bliley, Rev. Nicholas Martin, O.S.B., J.C.D., Altars According to the Code of Canon Law, XIX-132 pp., 1927.
39. Brown, Mr. Brendan Francis, A.B., LL.M., J.U.D., The Canonical Juristic Personality with Special Reference to its Status in the United States of America, V-212 pp., 1927.

40. CAVANAUGH, REV. WILLIAM THOMAS, C.P., J.U.D., The Reservation of the Blessed Sacrament, VIII-101 pp., 1927.
41. DOHENY, REV. WILLIAM J., C.S.C., A.B., J.U.D., Church Property: Modes of Acquisition, X-118 pp., 1927.
42. FELDHAUS, REV. ALOYSIUS H., C.PP.S., J.C.D., Oratories, IX-141 pp., 1927.
43. KELLY, REV. JAMES PATRICK, A.B., J.C.D., The Jurisdiction of the Simple Confessor, X-208 pp., 1927.
44. NEUBERGER, REV. NICHOLAS J., J.C.D., Canon 6 or the Relation of the Codex Juris Canonici to the Preceding Legislation, V-95 pp., 1927.
45. O'KEEFE, REV. GERALD MICHAEL, J.C.D., Matrimonial Dispensations, Powers of Bishops, Priests, and Confessors, VIII-232 pp., 1927.
46. QUIGLEY, REV. JOSEPH A. M., A.B., J.C.D., Condemned Societies, 139 pp., 1927.
47. ZAPLOTNIK, REV. JOHANNES LEO, J.C.D., De Vicariis Foraneis, X-142 pp., 1927.
48. DUSKIE, REV. JOHN ALOYSIUS, A.B., J.C.D., The Canonical Status of the Orientals in the United States, VIII-196 pp., 1928.
49. HYLAND, REV. FRANCIS EDWARD, J.C.D., Excommunication, Its Nature, Historical Development and Effects, VIII-181 pp., 1928.
50. REINMANN, REV. GERALD JOSEPH, O.M.C., J.C.D., The Third Order Secular of Saint Francis, 201 pp., 1928.
51. SCHENK, REV. FRANCIS J., J.C.D., The Matrimonial Impediments of Mixed Religion and Disparity of Cult, XVI-318 pp., 1929.
52. COADY, REV. JOHN JOSEPH, S.T.D., J.U.D., A.M., The Appointment of Pastors, VIII-150 pp., 1929.
53. KAY, REV. THOMAS HENRY, J.C.D., Competence in Matrimonial Procedure, VIII-164 pp., 1929.
54. TURNER, REV. SIDNEY JOSEPH, C.P., J.U.D., The Vow of Poverty, XLIX-217 pp., 1929.
55. KEARNEY, REV. RAYMOND A., A.B., S.T.D., J.C.D., The Principles of Delegation, VII-149 pp., 1929.
56. CONRAN, REV. EDWARD JAMES, A.B., J.C.D., The Interdict, V-163 pp., 1930.
57. O'NEILL, REV. WILLIAM H., J.C.D., Papal Rescripts of Favor, VII-218 pp., 1930.
58. BASTNAGEL, REV. CLEMENT VINCENT, J.U.D., The Appointment of Parochial Adjutants and Assistants, XV-257 pp., 1930.
59. FERRY, REV. WILLIAM A., A.B., J.C.D., Stole Fees, V-136 pp., 1930.
60. COSTELLO, REV. JOHN MICHAEL, A.B., J.C.D., Domicile and Quasi-Domicile, VII-201 pp., 1930.
61. KREMER, REV. MICHAEL NICHOLAS, A.B., S.T.B., J.C.D., Church Support in the United States, VI-136 pp., 1930.
62. ANGULO, REV. LUIS, C.M., J.C.D., Legislation de la Iglesia sobre la intencion en la application de la Santa Misa, VII-104 pp., 1931.

63. Frey, Rev. Wolfgang Norbert, O.S.B., A.B., J.C.D., The Act of Religious Profession, VIII-174 pp., 1931.
64. Roberts, Rev. James Brendan, A.B., J.C.D., The Banns of Marriage, XIV-140 pp., 1931.
65. Ryder, Rev. Raymond Aloysius, A.B., J.C.D., Simony, IX-151 pp., 1931.
66. Campagna, Rev. Angelo, Ph.D., J.U.D., Il Vicario Generale del Vescovo, VII-205 pp., 1931.
67. Cox, Rev. Joseph Godfrey, A.B., J.C.D., The Administration of Seminaries, VI-124 pp., 1931.
68. Gregory, Rev. Donald J., J.U.D., The Pauline Privilege, XV-165 pp., 1931.
69. Donohue, Rev. John F., J.C.D., The Impediment of Crime, VII-110 pp., 1931.
70. Dooley, Rev. Eugene A., O.M.I., J.C.D., Church Law on Sacred Relics, IX-143 pp., 1931.
71. Orth, Rev. Clement Raymond, O.M.C., J.C.D., The Approbation of Religious Institutes, 171 pp., 1931.
72. Pernicone, Rev. Joseph M., A.B., J.C.D., The Ecclesiastical Prohibition of Books, XII-267 pp., 1932.
73. Clinton, Rev. Connell, A.B., J.C.D., The Paschal Precept, IX-108 pp., 1932.
74. Donnelly, Rev. Francis B., A.M., S.T.L., J.C.D., The Diocesan Synod, VIII-125 pp., 1932.
75. Torrente, Rev. Camilo, C.M.F., J.C.D., Las Procesiones Sagradas, V-145 pp., 1932.
76. Murphy, Rev. Edwin J., C.PP.S., J.C.D., Suspension Ex Informata Conscientia, XI-122 pp., 1932.
77. MacKenzie, Rev. Eric F., A.M., S.T.L., J.C.D., The Delict of Heresy in its Commission, Penalization, Absolution, VII-124 pp., 1932.
78. Lyons, Rev. Avitus E., S.T.B., J.C.D., The Collegiate Tribunal of First Instance, XI-147 pp., 1932.
79. Connolly, Rev. Thomas A., J.C.D., Appeals, XI-195 pp., 1932.
80. Sangmeister, Rev. Joseph V., A.B., J.C.D., Force and Fear as Precluding Matrimonial Consent, V-211 pp., 1932.
81. Jaeger, Rev. Leo A., A.B., J.C.D., The Administration of Vacant and Quasi-Vacant Episcopal Sees in the United States, IX-229 pp., 1932.
82. Rimlinger, Rev. Herbert T., J.C.D., Error Invalidating Matrimonial Consent, VII-79 pp., 1932.
83. Barrett, Rev. John D. M., S.S., J.C.D., A Comparative Study of the Third Plenary Council of Baltimore and the Code, IX-221 pp., 1932.
84. Carberry, Rev. John J., Ph.D., S.T.D., J.C.D., The Juridical Form of Marriage, X-177 pp., 1934.
85. Dolan, Rev. John L., A.B., J.C.D., The Defensor Vinculi, XII-157 pp., 1934.

86. HANNAN, REV. JEROME D., A.M., S.T.D., LL.B., J.C.D., The Canon Law of Wills, IX-517 pp., 1934.
87. LEMIEUX, REV. DELISE A., A.M., J.C.D., The Sentence in Ecclesiastical Procedure, IX-131 pp., 1934.
88. O'ROURKE, REV. JAMES J., A.B., J.C.D., Parish Registers, VII-109 pp., 1934.
89. TIMLIN, REV. BARTHOLOMEW, O.F.M., A.M., J.C.D., Conditional Matrimonial Consent, X-381 pp., 1934.
90. WAHL, REV. FRANCIS X., A.B., J.C.D., The Matrimonial Impediments of Consanguinity and Affinity, VI-125 pp., 1934.
91. WHITE, REV. ROBERT J., A.B., LL.B., S.T.B., J.C.D., Canonical Ante-Nuptial Promises and the Civil Law, VI-152 pp., 1934.
92. HERRERA, REV. ANTONIO PARRA, O.C.D., J.C.D., Legislacion Ecclesiastica sobra el Ayuno y la Abstinencia, XI-191 pp., 1935.
93. KENNEDY, REV. EDWIN J., J.C.D., The Special Matrimonial Process in Cases of Evident Nullity, X-165 pp., 1935.
94. MANNING, REV. JOHN J., A.B., J.C.D., Presumption of Law in Matrimonial Procedure, XI-111 pp., 1935.
95. MOEDER, REV. JOHN M., J.C.D., The Proper Bishop for Ordination and Dimissorial Letters, VII-135 pp., 1935.
96. O'MARA, REV. WILLIAM A., A.B., J.C.D., Canonical Causes for Matrimonial Dispensations, IX-155 pp., 1935.
97. REILLY, REV. PETER, J.C.D., Residence of Pastors, IX-81 pp., 1935.
98. SMITH, REV. MARINER T., O.P., S.T.Lr., J.C.D., The Penal Law for Religious, VII-169 pp., 1935.
99. WHALEN, REV. DONALD W., A.M., J.C.D., The Value of Testimonial Evidence in Matrimonial Procedure, XIII-297 pp., 1935.
100. CLEARY, REV. JOSEPH F., J.C.D., Canonical Limitations on the Alienation of Church Property, VIII-141 pp., 1936.
101. GLYNN, REV. JOHN C., J.C.D., The Promoter of Justice, XX-337 pp., 1936.
102. BRENNAN, REV. JAMES H., S.S., M.A., S.T.B., J.C.D., The Simple Convalidation of Marriage, VI-135 pp., 1937.
103. BRUNINI, REV. JOSEPH BERNARD, J.C.D., The Clerical Obligations of Canons 139 and 142, X-121 pp., 1937.
104. CONNOR, REV. MAURICE, A.B., J.C.D., The Administrative Removal of Pastors, VIII-159 pp., 1937.
105. GUILFOYLE, REV. MERLIN JOSEPH, J.C.D., Custom, XI-144 pp., 1937.
106. HUGHES, REV. JAMES AUSTIN, A.B., A.M., J.C.D., Witnesses in Criminal Trials of Clerics, IX-140 pp., 1937.
107. JANSEN, REV. RAYMOND J., A.B., S.T.L., J.C.D., Canonical Provisions for Catechetical Instruction, VII-153 pp., 1937.
108. KEALY, REV. JOHN JAMES, A.B., J.C.D., The Introductory Libellus in Church Court Procedure, XI-121 pp., 1937.

109. McManus, Rev. James Edward, C.SS.R., J.C.D., The Administration of Temporal Goods in Religious Institutes, XVI-196 pp., 1937.
110. Moriarty, Rev. Eugene James, J.C.D., Oaths in Ecclesiastical Courts, X-115 pp., 1937.
111. Rainer, Rev. Eligius George, C.SS.R., J.C.D., Suspension of Clerics, XVII-249 pp., 1937.
112. Reilly, Rev. Thomas F., C.SS.R., J.C.D., Visitation of Religious, VI-195 pp., 1938.
113. Moriarity, Rev. Francis E., C.SS.R., J.C.D., The Extraordinary Absolution from Censures, XV-334 pp., 1938.
114. Connolly, Rev. Nicholas P., J.C.D., The Canonical Erection of Parishes, X-132 pp., 1938.
115. Donovan, Rev. James Joseph, J.C.D., The Pastor's Obligation in Prenuptial Investigation, XII-322 pp., 1938.
116. Harrigan, Rev. Robert J., M.A., S.T.B., J.C.D., The Radical Sanation of Invalid Marriages, VIII-208 pp., 1938.
117. Boffa, Rev. Conrad Humbert, J.C.D., Canonical Provisions for Catholic Schools, VII-211 pp., 1939.
118. Parsons, Rev. Anscar John, O.M.Cap., J.C.D., Canonical Elections, XII-236 pp., 1939.
119. Reilly, Rev. Edward Michael, A.B., J.C.D., The General Norms of Dispensation, XII-156 pp., 1939.
120. Ryan, Rev. Gerald Aloysius, A.B., J.C.D., Principles of Episcopal Jurisdiction, XII-172 pp., 1939.
121. Burton, Rev. Francis James, C.S.C., A.B., J.C.D., A Commentary on Canon 1125, X-222 pp., 1940.
122. Miaskiewicz, Rev. Francis Sigismund, J.C.D., Supplied Jurisdiction According to Canon 209, XII-340 pp., 1940.
123. Rice, Rev. Patrick William, A.B., J.C.D., Proof of Death in Prenuptial Investigation, VIII-156 pp., 1940.
124. Anglin, Rev. Thomas Francis, M.S., J.C.D., The Eucharistic Fast, VIII-183 pp., 1941.
125. Coleman, Rev. John Jerome, J.C.D., The Minister of Confirmation, VI-153 pp., 1941.
126. Downs, Rev. Joseph Emmanuel, A.B., J.C.D., The Concept of Clerical Immunity, XI-163 pp., 1941.
127. Esswein, Rev. Anthony Albert, J.C.D., Extrajudicial Penal Powers of Ecclesiastical Superiors, X-144 pp., 1941.
128. Farrell, Rev. Benjamin Francis, M.A., S.T.L., J.C.D., The Rights and Duties of the Local Ordinary Regarding Congregations of Women Religious of Pontifical Approval, V-195 pp., 1941.
129. Feeney, Rev. Thomas John, A.B., S.T.L., J.C.D., Restitutio in Integrum, VI-169 pp., 1941.
130. Findlay, Rev. Stephen William, O.S.B., A.B., J.C.D., Canonical

Norms Governing the Deposition and Degradation of Clerics, XVII-279 pp., 1941.

131. GOODWINE, REV. JOHN, A.B., S.T.L., J.C.D., The Right of the Church to Acquire Property, VIII-119 pp., 1941.
132. HESTON, REV. EDWARD LOUIS, C.S.C., Ph.D., S.T.D., J.C.D., The Alienation of Church Property in the United States, XII-222 pp., 1941.
133. HOGAN, REV. JAMES JOHN, A.B., S.T.L., J.C.D., Judicial Advocates and Procurators, XIII-200 pp., 1941.
134. KEALY, REV. THOMAS M., A.B., Litt.B., J.C.D., Dowry of Women Religious, IX-152 pp., 1941.
135. KEENE, REV. MICHAEL JAMES, O.S.B., J.C.D., Religious Ordinaries and Canon 198, V-164 pp., 1942.
136. KERIN, REV. CHARLES A., S.S., M.A., S.T.B., J.C.D., The Privation of Christian Burial, XVI-279 pp., 1941.
137. LOUIS, REV. WILLIAM FRANCIS, M.A., J.C.D., Diocesan Archives, X-101 pp., 1941.
138. McDEVITT, REV. GILBERT JOSEPH, A.B., J.C.D., Legitimacy and Legitimation, X-247 pp., 1941.
139. McDONOUGH, REV. THOMAS JOSEPH, A.B., J.C.D., Apostolic Administrators, X-217 pp., 1941.
140. MEIER, REV. CARL ANTHONY, A.B., J.C.D., Penal Administration Procedure Against Negligent Pastors, XI-240 pp., 1941.
141. SCHMIDT, REV. JOHN ROGG, A.B., J.C.D., The Principles of Authentic Interpretation in Canon 17 of the Code of Canon Law, XII-331 pp., 1941.
142. SLAFKOSKY, REV. ANDREW LEONARD, A.B., J.C.D., The Canonical Episcopal Visitation of the Diocese, X-197 pp., 1941.
143. SWOBODA, REV. INNOCENT ROBERT, O.F.M., J.C.D., Ignorance in Relation to the Imputability of Delicts, IX-271 pp., 1941.
144. DUBÉ, REV. ARTHUR JOSEPH, A.B., J.C.D., The General Principles for the Reckoning of Time in Canon Law, VIII-299 pp., 1941.
145. McBRIDE, REV. JAMES T., A.B., J.C.D., Incardination and Excardination of Seculars, XX-585 pp., 1941.
146 KRÓL, REV. JOHN T., J.C.D., The Defendant in Ecclesiastical Trials, XII-207 pp., 1942.
147. COMYNS, REV. JOSEPH J., C.SS.R., A.B., J.C.D., Papal and Episcopal Administration of Church Property, XIV-155 pp., 1942.
148. BARRY, REV. GARRETT FRANCIS, O.M.I., J.C.D., Violation of the Cloister, XII-260 pp., 1942.
149. BOLDUC, REV. GATIEN, C.S.V., A.B., S.T.L., J.C.D., Les Études dans les Religions Cléricales, VIII-155 pp., 1942.
150. BOYLE, REV. DAVID JOHN, M.A., J.C.D., The Juridic Effects of Moral Certitude on Pre-Nuptial Guarantees, XII-188 pp., 1942.
151. CANAVAN, REV. WALTER JOSEPH, M.A., LITT.D., J.C.D., The Profession of Faith, XII-143 pp., 1942.

152. Desrochers, Rev. Bruno, A.B., Ph.L., S.T.B., J.C.D., Le Premier Concile Plénier de Québec et le Code de Droit Canonique, XIV-186 pp., 1942.

153. Dillon, Rev. Robert Edward, A.B., J.C.D., Common Law Marriage, X-148 pp., 1942.

154. Dodwell, Rev. Edward John, Ph.D., S.T.B., J.C.D., The Time and Place for the Celebration of Marriage, X-156 pp., 1942.

155. Donnellan, Rev. Thomas Andrew, A.B., J.C.D., The Obligation of the Missa pro Populo, VII-131 pp., 1942.

156. Eltz, Rev. Louis Anthony, A.B., J.C.D., Cooperation in Crime, XII-208 pp., 1942.

157. Gass, Rev. Sylvester Francis, M.A., J.C.D., Ecclesiastical Pensions, XI-206 pp., 1942.

158. Guiniven, Rev. John Joseph, C.SS.R., J.C.D., The Precept of Hearing Mass, XIV-188 pp., 1942.

159. Gulczynski, Rev. John Theophilus, J.C.D., The Desecration and Violation of Churches, X-126 pp., 1942.

160. Hammill, Rev. John Leo, M.A., J.C.D., The Obligations of the Traveler According to Canon 14, VIII-204 pp., 1942.

161. Haydt, Rev. John Joseph, A.B., J.C.D., Reserved Benefices, XI-148 pp., 1942.

162. Huser, Rev. Roger John, O.F.M., A.B., J.C.D., The Crime of Abortion in Canon Law, XII-187 pp., 1942.

163. Kearney, Rev. Francis Patrick, A.B., S.T.L., J.C.L., The Principles of Canon 1127.

164. Linahen, Rev. Leo James, S.T.L., J.C.D., De Absolutione Complicis In Peccato Turpi, 114 pp., 1942.

165. McCloskey, Rev. Joseph Aloysius, A.B., J.C.D., The Subject of Ecclesiastical Law According to Canon 12, XVII-246 pp., 1942.

166. O'Neill, Rev. Francis Joseph, C.SS.R., J.C.D., The Dismissal of Religious in Temporary Vows, XIII-220 pp., 1942.

167. Prince, Rev. John Edward, A.B., S.T.D., J.C.D., The Diocesan Chancellor, X-136 pp., 1942.

168. Riesner, Rev. Albert Joseph, C.SS.R., J.C.D., Apostates and Fugitives from Religious Institutes, IX-168 pp., 1942.

169. Stenger, Rev. Joseph Bernard, J.C.D., The Mortgaging of Church Property, 186 pp., 1942.

170. Waldron, Rev. Joseph Francis, A.B., J.C.D., The Minister of Baptism, XII-197 pp., 1942.

171. Willett, Rev. Robert Albert, J.C.D., The Probative Value of Documents in Ecclesiastical Trials, X-124 pp., 1942.

172. Woeber, Rev. Edward Martin, M.A., J.C.D., The Interpellations, XII-161 pp., 1942.

173. Benko, Rev. Matthew Aloysius, O.S.B., M.A., J.C.D., The Abbot *Nullius*, XIV-148 pp., 1943.

174. CHRIST, REV. JOSEPH JAMES, M.A., S.T.L., J.C.D., Dispensation from Vindicative Penalties, XIV-285 pp., 1943.
175. CLANCY, REV. PATRICK M. J., O.P., A.B., S.T.LR., J.C.D., The Local Religious Superior, X-229 pp., 1943.
176. CLARKE, REV. THOMAS JAMES, J.C.D., Parish Societies, XII-147 pp., 1943.
177. CONNOLLY, REV. JOHN PATRICK, S.T.L., J.C.D., Synodal Examiners and Parish Priest Consultors, X-223 pp., 1943.
178. DRUMM, REV. WILLIAM MARTIN, A.B., J.C.D., Hospital Chaplains, XII-175 pp., 1943.
179. FLANAGAN, REV. BERNARD JOSEPH, A.B., S.T.L., J.C.D., The Canonical Erection of Religious Houses, X-147 pp., 1943.
180. KELLEHER, REV. STEPHEN JOSEPH, A.B., S.T.B., J.C.D., Discussions with non-Catholics: Canonical Legislation, X-93 pp., 1943.
181. LEWIS, REV. GORDIAN, C.P., J.C.D., Chapters in Religious Institutes, XII-169 pp., 1943.
182. MARX, REV. ADOLPH, J.C.D., The Declaration of Nullity of Marriages Contracted Outside the Church, X-151 pp., 1943.
183. MATULENAS, REV. RAYMOND ANTHONY, O.S.B., A.B., J.C.L., Communication, a Source of Privileges, XII-225 pp., 1943.
184. O'LEARY, REV. CHARLES GERARD, C.SS.R., J.C.D., Religious Dismissed After Perpetual Profession, X-213 pp., 1943.
185. POWER, REV. CORNELIUS MICHAEL, J.C.D., The Blessing of Cemeteries, XII-231 pp., 1943.
186. SHUHLER, REV. RALPH VINCENT, O.S.A., J.C.D., Privileges of Regulars to Absolve and Dispense, XII-195 pp., 1943.
187. ZIOLKOWSKI, REV. THADDEUS STANISLAUS, A.B., J.C.D., The Consecration and Blessing of Churches, XII-151 pp., 1943.
188. HENEGHAN, REV. JOHN JOSEPH, S.T.D., J.C.D., The Marriages of Unworthy Catholics: Canons 1065 and 1066, XVI-213 pp., 1944.
189. CARROLL, REV. COLEMAN FRANCIS, M.A., S.T.L., J.C.L., Charitable Institutions.
190. CIESLUK, REV. JOSEPH EDWARD, Ph.B., S.T.L., J.C.L., National Parishes in the United States.
191. COBURN, REV. VINCENT PAUL, A.B., J.C.D., Marriages of Conscience, XII-172 pp., 1944.
192. CONNORS, REV. CHARLES PAUL, C.S.Sp., A.B., J.C.L., Extra-Judicial Procurators in the Code of Canon Law, X-94 pp., 1944.
193. COYLE, REV. PAUL RAYMOND, A.B., J.C.L., Judicial Exceptions.
194. FAIR, REV. BARTHOLOMEW FRANCIS, A.B., S.T.L., J.C.L., The Impediment of Abduction.
195. GALLAGHER, REV. THOMAS RAPHAEL, O.P., A.B., S.T.Lr., J.C.L., The Examination of the Qualities of the Ordinand, X-166 pp., 1944.
196. GANNON, REV. JOHN MARK, S.T.L., J.C.L., The Interstices Required for the Promotion to Orders, XII-100 pp., 1944.

197. GOLDSMITH, REV. J. WILLIAM, B.C.S., S.T.L., J.C.L., The Competence of Church and State over Marriage—Disputed Points, X-128 pp., 1944.
198. GOODWINE, REV. JOSEPH GERARD, A.B., S.T.B., J.C.L., The Reception of Converts, XIV-326 pp., 1944.
199. KOWALSKI, REV. ROMUALD EUGENE, O.F.M., A.B., J.C.D., Sustenance of Religious Houses of Regulars, X-174 pp., 1944.
200. McCOY, REV. ALAN EDWARD, O.F.M., J.C.D., Force and Fear in Relation to Delictual Imputability and Penal Responsibility, XII-160 pp., 1944.
201. McDEVITT, REV. VINCENT JOHN, Ph.B., S.T.L., J.C.L., Perjury.
202. MARTIN, REV. THOMAS OWEN, Ph.D., S.T.D., J.C.D., Adverse Possession, Prescription and Limitation of Actions: The Canonical "Praescriptio," XX-208 pp., 1944.
203. MIKLOSOVIC, REV. PAUL JOHN, A.B., J.C.L., Attempted Marriages and Their Consequent Juridic Effects.
204. MUNDY, REV. THOMAS MAURICE, A.B., S.T.L., J.C.L., The Union of Parishes.
205. O'DEA, REV. JOHN COYLE, A.B., J.C.D., The Matrimonial Impediment of Nonage, VIII-126 pp., 1944.
206. OLALIA, REV. ALEXANDER AYSON, S.T.L., J.C.D., A Comparative Study of the Christian Constitution of States and the Constitution of the Philippine Commonwealth, XII, 136 pp., 1944.
207. POISSON, REV. PIERRE-MARIE, C.S.C., A.B., Ph.L., Th.L., J.C.L., Droits Patrimoniaux des Maisons et des Églises Religieuses.
208. STADALNIKAS, REV. CASIMIR JOSEPH, M.I.C., J.C.D., Reservation of Censures, X-141 pp., 1944.
209. SULLIVAN, REV. EUGENE HENRY, S.T.L., J.C.L., Proof of the Reception of the Sacraments.
210. VAUGHAN, REV. WILLIAM EDWARD, J.C.D., Constitutions for Diocesan Courts, X-210 pp., 1944.
211. PARO, REV. GINO, S.T.D., J.C.L., The Right of Apostolic Delegation.
212. BALZER, REV. RALPH FRANCIS, C.P., J.C.L., The Computation of Time in a Canonical Novitiate.
213. DOUGHERTY, REV. JOHN WHELAN, A.B., S.T.L., J.C.L., De Inquisitione Speciali.
214. DZIOB, REV. MICHAEL WALTER, J.C.L., The Sacred Congregation for the Oriental Church.
215. EIDENSCHINK, REV. JOHN ALBERT, O.S.B., B.A., J.C.L., The Election of Bishops in the Letters of Pope Gregory the Great.
216. GILL, REV. NICHOLAS, C.P., J.C.L., The Spiritual Prefect in Clerical Religious Houses of Study.
217. HYNES, REV. HARRY GERARD, S.T.L., J.C.L., The Privileges of Cardinals.
218. McDEVITT, REV. GERALD VINCENT, S.T.L., J.C.L., The Renunciation of an Ecclesiastical Office.

219. MANNING, REV. JOSEPH LEROY, J.C.L., The Free Conferral of Offices.
220. MEYER, REV. LOUIS G., O.S.B., A.B., S.T.B., J.C.L., Alms-Gathering by Religious.
221. O'DONNELL, REV. CLETUS FRANCIS, M.A., J.C.L., The Marriage of Minors.
222. PRUNSKIS, REV. JOSEPH, J.C.L., Comparative Law, Ecclesiastical and Civil, in Lithuanian Concordat.
223. SWEENEY, REV. FRANCIS PATRICK, C.Ss.R., J.C.L., The Reduction of Clerics to the Lay State.
224. VOGELPOHL, REV. HENRY JOHN, J.C.L., The Simple Impediments to Holy Orders.

www.ingramcontent.com/pod-product-compliance
Lightning Source LLC
LaVergne TN
LVHW050227080826
844660LV00012B/487

* 9 7 8 0 8 1 3 2 2 4 0 4 6 *